Jonathan Jennings

Indiana's First Governor

Artist James Forbes's portrait of Indiana governor Jonathan Jennings.

INDIANA BIOGRAPHY SERIES

Jonathan Jennings
Indiana's First Governor

RANDY K. MILLS

GENERAL EDITORS

RAY E. BOOMHOWER, KATHLEEN M. BREEN, AND PAULA J. CORPUZ

INDIANA HISTORICAL SOCIETY PRESS

INDIANAPOLIS 2005

Printed in Canada

This book is a publication of the
Indiana Historical Society Press
450 West Ohio Street
Indianapolis, Indiana 46202-3269 USA
www.indianahistory.org
Telephone orders 1-800-447-1830
Fax orders 317-234-0562
Order online @ shop.indianahistory.org

Library of Congress Cataloging-in-Publication Data

Mills, Randy Keith, 1951-

　Jonathan Jennings : Indiana's first governor / Randy K. Mills.
　　p. cm. — (Indiana biography series)
　Includes bibliographical references.
　ISBN 0-87195-182-7 (cloth : alk. paper)
　　1. Jennings, Jonathan, 1784–1834. 2. Governors—Indiana—
Biography. 3. Indiana—Politics and government—19th century. 4.
Legislators—United States—Biography. 5. United States. Congress.
House—Biography. I. Title. II. Series.

F526.J46M55 2005
977.2'03'092—dc22
　[B]
2005047490

Dedicated to my wife and companion, Roxanne.

TABLE OF CONTENTS

A C K N O W L E D G M E N T S

THE CONSTRUCTION OF A BOOK IS NEVER ACCOMPLISHED alone. I wish to recognize here the many people who have been a part of making this book possible. To the staff at the Indiana Historical Society Press—especially Tom Mason, Ray Boomhower, Paula Corpuz, Kathy Breen, and Rachel Popma—I offer a heartfelt thank you. I also wish to acknowledge Dr. Bruce Bigelow at Butler University for his many thoughts regarding the early cultural history of Indiana, and especially for his insights concerning the influence of settlers from southwestern Pennsylvania on frontier Indiana.

A number of library staffs provided research material and suggestions where hard-to-find resources might be located. I wish to thank the staff at the Indiana Historical Society's William Henry Smith Memorial Library; the Indiana State Library; Special Collections, Willard Library, Evansville, Indiana; Oakland City University Library; Lewis

Library, Vincennes University; Indiana University Library, including the Lilly Special Collections Library; University of Southern Indiana Library; Oakland City Columbia Township Public Library; Princeton Public Library; and Jasper Public Library.

For typing and research work I wish to thank Angie Carlen. Angie also offered timely editorial suggestions. Another typing aid was Andy Mills—thanks Andy.

A Lilly Endowment grant, gained through Oakland City University, allowed me extra time to carry out essential research for this project—time that I would not typically have had. I deeply appeciate the help of both the Lilly Endowment and the administration at the university, especially Dr. James W. Murray and Dr. Bernard Marley.

My wife, Roxanne Mills, provided early copyediting, as well as many helpful editorial comments. Mostly, I wish to thank her for her consistent support and encouragement.

as a champion of the common man, and as the leader of the state's antislavery contingent. In *Indiana: A Redemption from Slavery*, Jacob P. Dunn Jr. described Jennings in almost mythical proportions as a "young Hercules, stripped for the fray, and wielding the mighty bludgeon of 'No slavery in Indiana.'"[5] While less dramatic, a decade earlier biographer William Woollen said of Jennings, "Indiana owes him more than she can compute. He fought slavery to the death when it sought to fasten itself upon her territory; he helped secure for her sons and daughters the best portion of her rich and fertile lands."[6] In 1877 John Nowland judged Jennings "an able statesman," while Indiana governor Samuel Ralston

Illustration used as part of Indiana's centennial celebration in 1916 showing the state seal and governors Jonathan Jennings and Samuel M. Ralston.

labeled Jennings "the fittest man to be his state's first governor."[7] Another observer further recognized Jennings's gifts
in the area of politics. Oliver H. Smith, a contemporary of
Jennings, offered this rather balanced appraisal: "His great
forte, like that of Martin Van Buren, was in managing the
wires that controlled popular elections. Still, he was by no
means destitute of talents. His messages read well, and he
made a useful business member of Congress. As a public
speaker he was not admired, but on paper he was a very
formidable competitor."[8]

Perhaps the strangest positive assessment of Jennings
can be found in William Cockrum's *A Pioneer History
of Indiana*, published in 1907. Cockrum, a well-known
supporter of the Prohibition movement in southwest
Indiana, related a story about Jennings's success in helping a neighbor to stop drinking. According to Cockrum,
Jennings often told the story of Tom Oglesby, a boyhood
friend from Pennsylvania, who Jennings supposedly told
while running for governor, "you are a finished civil engi-
neer and very well educated, if you will quit drinking, I
will see that you have a good place on the surveying
corps." Cockrum asserted, "Tom Oglesby did quit drinking, Jennings was elected and put his old school mate in
the engineerig [*sic*] department, and he became one of
the greatest engineers in the United States."[9] At the time
of Cockrum's writing, Jennings's drinking problems were
rarely stressed. However, that soon changed.

the height of Prohibition, a time when the nation's general attitude concerning drinking was extremely negative. In Jennings's day, Rorabaugh noted, drinking commonly occurred "whenever groups of Americans gathered for elections, court sessions, militia musters, holiday celebrations, or neighborly festivities. Practically any gathering . . . provided an occasion for drinking vast qualities of liquor, until the more prudent staggered home while the remainder quarreled and fought, or passed out."[20] It was simply no great shame to drink large amounts of intoxicants. Indeed, people living in frontier areas such as Indiana, perhaps more than any other region of the nation, consumed great quantities of alcohol, especially distilled whiskey. A New York visitor to Vincennes, where Jennings himself settled for a while, noted that "Whisky is drunk like water. . . . Men drink it by the quart & even the wealthy prefer it to any of the foreign liquors."[21] Even religious bodies, such as the frontier Baptists, unaware of alcohol's effect on addicts, often paid their ministers with whiskey by the gallon.[22] At important frontier social events whiskey was offered to every man, woman, and child.

The problem was even more pronounced among Native American groups on the frontier. Territorial governor William Henry Harrison complained in an 1801 letter, for example, of the great problems caused by local Indian groups when they drank: "They are dayly in this town in considerable numbers and are frequently intoxicated to the number of thirty or forty at once—they then commit the greatest disorders—drawing their knives and stabing every one they meet with—breaking open the Houses of the Citizens killing their Hogs and cattle and breaking down their fences. But in all their frolicks they generally suffer most severely themselves they kill each other without mercy."[23] That same year Harrison issued an executive proclamation forbidding traders from "selling or giving away spirituous Liquors to any Indian or Indians in the town of Vincennes." In that same proclamation it is also apparent that the problem included white settlers as well. The official order went on to decree that "all Magistrates and other Civil officers [are] vigilantly to discharge their duties, by punishing, as the Law directs, all persons who are found drunk, or rioting in the streets or public houses."[24]

Demonstrating the lack of understanding at that time regarding alcohol's power over those who possessed a tendency toward addiction, Harrison, in another letter written during the same period, inquired about his own whiskey distillery, adding, "I wish you to send me some Whiskey as soon as possible."[25] Jennings also had his own distillery later in his life when he lived near Charlestown. Unfortunately for Jennings, alcohol also played a powerful role in frontier political contests. A hopeful candidate was expected to hardily "treat" potential voters and, if he was truly a man of the people, take several swigs of the jug himself. Further, any political discussion at a local tavern or inn or at any other pioneer social event likely included an ample supply of alcohol. One frontier citizen from Evansville complained of this common practice by observing that "during an election campaign the idle and intemperate repair to places of public resort, in hope of finding more candidates who will give them a liberal price in whisky for their votes. . . . How often is the eye of sober sense disgusted at the low, groveling, sycophantic conduct of candidates, and how often is the genuine ear of republicanism punished at the savage yells and huzzas of [drunken] voters for a candidate on the eve and day of election."[26] Obviously election time would have been an especially difficult period for anyone such as Jennings who struggled with a drinking problem.

Another compelling reason for inquiring about the life of this complex man is that to speak of Jennings is to speak of frontier politics. Early Hoosiers often referred to the practice of politics as electioneering and understood that the endeavor included both an idealistic level of commitment to certain American political principles and a lower level of rough-and-tumble, no-holds-barred activities. Unbridled ambition and personal pride often played a key role in this process as well, as a letter penned by Samuel Judah, a Jennings contemporary, suggests. Judah, writing a longtime political adversary in his own party about running for office, asserted, "By some It is said that

you are a candidate for re-election. . . . be that as it may
. . . it seems to me that I have given way often enough. . . .
I have determined to be a candidate." Judah then boldly
declared, "I owe some thing to myself . . . some thing too
is due to my own feelings."[27]

Jennings himself was not unaware of the dark side of
electioneering, writing once in a moment of candor, "politicks are noisy deceptive subjects."[28] Yet given this suggested distaste for political endeavors, perhaps no other
frontier Hoosier played the political game as well as
Jennings. For this reason, an examination of his life and
political career offers the potential for great insight into
the realities of early American frontier politics.

The noise and bustle of intense political activity represented one of the major elements of early American
life, with frontier regions apparently containing more
political passion and commotion than other areas of the
nation. A former New Englander living in Indiana, Calvin
Fletcher, noted in his diary that citizens of the Hoosier
State "are bold & independent in their sentiments as to
public men or measures. The most ignorant man here
knows who governs him & who administers justice."
Conversely, Fletcher observed, "In N[ew] E[ngland], the
governments are becoming arrestcratical & the common
people put all credence in great men."[29]

On a national level, early visitors to this country often
shuddered at Americans' intense, almost maniacal inter-

est in politics and elections. "No sooner do you set foot upon American ground," noted an astounded Alexis de Tocqueville, "than you are stunned by a kind of tumult; a confused clamor is heard on every side, and a thousand simultaneous voices demand the satisfaction of their social wants." Americans' extreme interest in all things political set, according to de Tocqueville, "Everything in motion around you; here the people of one quarter of a town are met to decide upon the building of a church; there the election of a representative is going on; a little farther, the delegates of a district are hastening to the town in order to consult upon some local improvements; in another place, the laborers of a village quit their plows to deliberate upon the project of a road or a public school. Meetings are called for the sole purpose of declaring their disapprobation of the conduct of the government."[30] Frances Trollope also spoke despairingly of the nation's "electioneering madness," which made her wish to "fly it in disgust." American politics, she asserted, "engrosses every conversation, it irritates every temper . . . and in fact, vitiates the whole system of society."[31]

De Tocqueville's even lower opinion regarding frontier politics blazed forth as especially damning. The Frenchman fretted over what he perceived to be the lack of political sophistication among citizens of frontier sectors. Speaking specifically of the Indiana region, de Tocqueville lamented that the settlers who streamed into this area were "in every respect, inferior to the Americans who inhabit the older parts of the Union. But they already exercise a great influence in its councils; and they arrive at the government of the commonwealth before they have learned to govern themselves."[32]

An English visitor to southern Indiana, in a series of letters to the *Evansville Gazette*, strongly concurred with de Tocqueville's view, observing, "Where judges, associates, sheriff, clerk, coroner, magistrate, commissioners, etc., from the highest to the least, are elected in a general election, it is impossible that these offices should be generally well filled. The whole system is ridiculous and exposes the people constantly to the risk of having the most important" positions given to "persons utterly unqualified . . . merely on account of their general popularity."[33] In another letter the same author asserted, "The people of Indiana [possess] a fondness for [political] offices . . . not exceeded by any other people under the sun."[34] Americans, especially frontiersmen, took little notice of these charges of political hyperactivity and a lack of political refinement. In the case of the forthright Englishman, whose letters to the *Gazette* were being carried in serial form, his correspondence was abruptly dropped by the paper. Foreign observers, however, had struck upon one powerful truth: Americans, especially frontiersmen, loved their politics, and among the best politicians stood Jennings.

Despite Jennings's frequent successes, however, he occasionally faced difficult opposition. Jennings's most troublesome political antagonist was none other than territorial governor Harrison. Notwithstanding Jennings's constant attacks against Harrison's proslavery and aristocratic policies, the governor remained a popular figure in Indiana until leaving his post in 1812. Much of his

William Henry Harrison

renown had to do with his attractive personality, along with his military leadership. The latter stood at a supremely important commodity at a time when settlers were under constant threat by Native American tribes. Jennings was never able to completely overthrow the governor, though this particular mission remained a constant endeavor throughout much of his early political life.

At age forty-seven, Jennings, beset by alcoholism, lost his seat in Congress. The former governor was now under constant financial strain. The hard drinking had, by this time, taken a toll on his health as well as his reputation. The next year William Polke, in a letter to Tipton, referred to Jennings as being "old" and worried that the former governor's drinking habit threatened to cause him to "be throwed by as useless."[35] Jennings, at the relatively young age of fifty, died at his farm in Clark County, Indiana, on July 26, 1832.

Like all politicians of his day, Jennings was a complex, all too human person possessing a multitude of inconsistencies. For reasons that have, until this project, remained unclear, historians have been generally unkind in their judgments regarding the place Jennings should hold in the state's history. This work, using not only previous sketches but also personal letters, official government records, and newspaper and diary accounts, seeks to present a more thorough and balanced assessment of

Indiana's first governor, as well as to provide insight into what Jennings was like as a person. It is hoped this study will better illuminate an important period of Indiana and American history as well, a time when "electioneering madness" was a major feature of American life.

A SPECIAL NOTE: *It is essential for readers to understand that references to Republicanism and the Republican Party in this work refer to the Jeffersonian Democratic-Republican Party and not the modern Republican Party. Later, followers of Jefferson dropped the Republican name and became the Democratic Party. See Paul Goodman, ed.,* The Federalists vs. the Jeffersonian Republicans *(New York: Holt, Rinehart and Company, 1967).*

1

"While other men make their fate"

SOCIAL SCIENTISTS HAVE LONG DEBATED THE ISSUE OF environment versus heredity. In the case of Jonathan Jennings, both elements played significant roles. Jennings himself seemed keenly aware of the environmental aspect, as he once wrote as a young adult of the circumstance regarding the loss of his mother when he was just seven years old. He observed his progress in life "would have been more advan[ced]" had his loving mother not have died at that time.[1] In a later observation, assessing his time as governor in 1826, Jennings noted that "fate makes some men while other men make their fate."[2] Jennings likely never understood his own genetic disposition toward alcoholism, a disease that plagued him in his later years, shortened his life, and led him to receive a negative assessment from historians. In the beginning, however, there were plenty of environmental problems for the young Jennings to face and

overcome—problems that greatly shaped his later feelings and actions.

Jennings's parents had strong ties to both the more
cultured region of the East Coast and the bleak frontier
area to the west. Jonathan's father, Jacob Jennings, was
the son of English-born parents who had settled in Long
Island, New York, before moving permanently to New
Jersey. Jacob was born in the latter colony in 1744. Both
Jacob's intelligence and keen sense of service to
humankind is suggested by the fact that he earned a medical degree at a time when most doctors learned medicine
as apprentices. In the process of securing his medical
training, he met and married Mary Kennedy (born 1749),
who may have also held a medical degree. Although little
is known about her early family background, it seems that
she too was committed to educational improvement and
service. All the Jennings sons were encouraged to pursue
an education, a rare choice in those days, especially on
the fringe of the western frontier where the Jennings
family eventually came to live.[3]

Some sense of the environmental dynamics of
Jonathan Jennings's early life can be acquired by looking
at the birth order of the Jennings family. Jacob and Mary's
first child, Sarah, was born in 1770, fourteen years before
Jonathan. The elder Jennings was already twenty-six years
old when his first daughter came into the colonial
American world. Samuel Kennedy arrived a year later.

Two years passed before another son, Jacob, was born. Ebenezer was born two years after Jacob, then another son, Obadiah, three years after that. There would then be a six-year break before Jonathan Jennings's own birth occurred in 1784. Hardly a year had passed when another daughter, Jonathan's beloved sister Ann, was born. Finally, a son, David, came three years following Jonathan's own birth.[4]

Several difficulties may have emerged for Jonathan from this early family circumstance. Jacob would have been forty years old at the time of his son's birth. He would have been considered old by that day's standards (the average life expectancy was less than forty years of age). The elder Jennings was also likely emotionally and physically drained from seeing after the five older siblings, causing him to have had little to offer Jonathan in the way of guidance or emotional support. The same could have been said for Mary, who shortly after Jonathan's birth became pregnant with Ann. In such circumstances, Jonathan was doubtlessly squeezed out of much-needed attention and emotional support from his mother as well. A result of this situation was that Jonathan suffered intense bouts of loneliness as an adult.

Under these difficult conditions, older brothers and sisters often become much like parents to younger siblings. This seems to be especially true in terms of Jonathan's relationship with his brother Ebenezer, who was nine years older. When Jonathan received news in 1808 that Ebenezer was dying of tuberculosis, he wrote a family member: "The unfavorable news of the event of my mercantile project was of little account, compared with the melancholy intelligence of Brother E. Jennings's irrevocable fate." The younger brother was moved to remember a recent time when Ebenezer had "stood over my *expected* Death Bed, with an unremitted attention." Jonathan went on to lament, "would to God that I could watch his declining days, his departing moments, and take his last assurance of the friendship of which his heart was so susceptible. Tell him if he yet lives, tell him for me, that my circumstances are such that I cannot again see him, until we shall meet at the Bar of Almighty God! Tell him a long farewell; bid a long, a sad & last adieu for a Brother who holds him near to his heart."[5]

The most defining event in Jonathan's young life was the death of his mother Mary, who, like so many women on the frontier, just simply wore out and died. One typical woman on the Old Northwest frontier wrote of a life "so hard, [with] so much to do, so pitiful little to do with."[6] Mary's death left a void in Jonathan that was never completely filled. To compensate for this tragic loss, the seven-year-old quickly developed an extraordinarily strong bond with his younger sister Ann. In a letter written when Jennings was thirty-three, he noted how his sister "was the constant companion of my childhood for many years, and

to me, is very, very dear." In the same letter, perhaps
moved to depression on thinking about the difficulties of
his youth, Jennings observed how man "expects much and
realizes little in this life but anxiety, pain and fatigue."[7]

When his beloved Ann married David G. Mitchell, a
physician, in 1806, Jennings, twenty-two years old and still
unmarried himself, sent his sister and his new brother-in-
law a lengthy letter offering advice on maintaining marital
bliss. To the groom, Jennings declared, "consider me as
addressing one closely connected to her that is as yet as
dear to me as any on this earth. Whilst I from my inmost
heart fervently desire that you both may enjoy every comfort and heartfelt satisfaction, this world can afford, suffer
me to transmit you a few desultory thoughts and selfmade
observations." Jennings then proceeded to address his sister, warning her "in every condition in life lively hopes of
futurity, and chilling blasts of adversity rise in thick succes-
sion; Thus at one time we are borne through all the
enchanting scenes of the unknown mazes of fruitful imag-
ination: anon we are by some trifling and unknown contin-
gency enveloped in clouds of black disappointment. The
only preventitive to corroding cares that I have found is
not to set too high an estimate on any prospect nor repine
at the blessings of the day."[8] By not hoping for much,
Jennings asserted, one could be better satisfied with what
little happiness life provided. It is a notion that suggests
much about his own inner turmoil.

To his new brother-in-law, Jennings related his ideas regarding being a successful husband. "Mitchell," wrote Jennings, "you as well as myself know that human nature is prone to err, that persons of nice feelings, are generally persons of warm passions. That the marriage state frees no one from the bonds of nature." Jennings then elaborated on how human nature, if not confronted, could easily lead to marital problems. "In the circle of my acquaintance there lives a young married couple," he wrote, "for some time after wedlock they seldom had any cause of contention, but now when anything ruffles the temper of the wife, she immediately finds fault with her husband, he impatient of being chid when conscious of no fault, retorts, and now by long custom, every month or two I am informed they will scarcely speak to each other for a week." Jennings went on to note that he knew "those who after marriage have lived years together, as happy as happy could be, afterward lived miserably all their lives." The concerned Jennings then proposed a remedy for the problem: "Let me offer this one thing to you as being the most able to affect it, [that] is, be sure the first [time] any coolness takes place, as there always does sooner or later between man and wife, remove the cause instantly and instead of having bad effects, it will tend rather to cement your affections."[9]

Finally, Jennings speaks of his unusual closeness to his sister to Mitchell as the reason for the rather intimate letter: "Now, Sir, to your care friend and husband I commit from henceforth, my only my beloved sister, the dearest relict of a once tender though departed mother, whom had she lived to bless her and myself with maternal [care], our [progress] in this life would have been more advan[ced]."[10] Apparently, Mitchell and Ann both took offence, for a month later Jennings wrote back to the couple to apologize. "Yours per mail came duly to hand, but let me inform you that if in my former I wrote any thing unpleasant to the feelings of either of you, I assure you that it was not intentionally," said Jennings. "Believe me, that I desire your happiness as well, and equally with my own. You are dear to me Sir, not only because you possess a generous and independant mind, but likewise that you are dear to her who has always been the tender object of my heart."[11] Ironically, Jennings apparently struggled with his own relationship problems at this time. "I should be glad [if] you would inform me," Jennings wrote Mitchell in a rather cryptic note a month after giving his brother-in-law marital advice, "if Miss Mahan has written Mama, and what Miss Nancy [Breading] thinks of my deserting her."[12]

Another powerful shaping force in Jonathan's early life was his father's extreme commitment to religion. Jacob had moved his family to a farm in New Jersey after receiving bounty land there for his service as a surgeon in the Revolutionary War. Mary's father was a Presbyterian minister in New Jersey, and Jacob soon became heavily involved in that rather rigid denomination as well. In the late 1700s the Presbyterians, especially the more evangelical "new light" wing, called for more missionary work in the less religious frontier areas of Virginia. Jacob answered that call as a doctor and missionary for the Dutch Reformed Church, another rather rigid denomination, in remote Hardy County, Virginia. Jonathan was likely born on the Virginia frontier during his father's missionary work there.

Five years after Jonathan's birth, his family returned to New Jersey, where the elder Jennings sought and received ordination in the Dutch Reformed Church. In 1792 Jacob Jennings came back to the Presbyterians and quickly took a church in Fayette County in southwest Pennsylvania, on the fringe of what was then the frontier. Here eight-year-old Jonathan spent the next fourteen years of his life. As a result, young Jennings learned much about frontier life and people, a knowledge he put to use once he settled in Indiana. The family's religious environment in Pennsylvania, however, may have had a negative effect on Jonathan. Jacob's strong religious convictions seemed to have emotionally overwhelmed Jonathan, causing him to reject organized religion in order to preserve his own spiritual identity. Jonathan's correspondence clearly indicates that he struggled his entire life regarding his own sense of spiritual fulfillment. When Jennings was twenty-nine years old, he wrote Mitchell, sharing with his brother-in-law that he had "often wished and sometimes determined to become a christian or at least to try."[13] No record of him doing so exists. Shortly after the deaths of his wife and his sister, Jennings wrote again to Mitchell about religion, observing, "religion is no chimera," but he still wished to be "a subject of its influence."[14]

One biographer, Brent Smith, blasts Jennings's seeming lack of resolve in this area, asserting, perhaps unfairly, the following:

> On a personal level, Jonathan Jennings was a frustrated individual, a man who fell short of the high spiritual expectations of his evangelical origins. Driven by the memory of an authoritarian father who stressed achievement educationally as well as spiritually, Jennings never quite measured up against his three older brothers. He submitted to a life of compromise, always planning to do the "right thing" and to become a Christian someday, but never grasping the concept of the grace of God in his life that would have enabled him to live the life he desired. The defect in his character was one of weakness. He lacked the commitment necessary to search out the spiritual void in his life, choosing the easier route of living with the insecurity rather than settling it.[15]

In fairness to Jennings, the practice of religion on the Indiana frontier often witnessed a great outpouring of emotions, a custom the more educated and reflective Jennings may have found wanting. These displays were quite something to behold. An English traveler through the area, for example, told of observing one Hoosier frontier minister in action. The preacher, Englishman William Faux reported, "stripped at it, taking off coat, waistcoat, and cravat, unbuttoning his shirt collar, and wildly throwing about his arms. He made the maddest gesticulations, for the space of two hours, ever seen in a man professing sanity."[16]

Another interesting element emerges in the early correspondences between Jennings and Mitchell that adds insight into Jennings's later drinking problems—the possible existence of alcoholism in the Jennings family. Studies have shown that this disease can be genetic. In an 1806 letter to Mitchell, Jennings bemoaned the problems caused by apparent alcohol abuse on the part of one of his nephews, Sarah's son Samuel Kennedy Simonson. Ironically, given the fact that Jennings himself would one day have the illness, he was highly judgmental of the young man and his drinking problems. After mentioning the turmoil created in the family by his nephew's misuse of alcohol, Jennings declared, "this much may be said with justice, that he is a great villain, that he is a great liar, that he is very artful and designing, that he may yet be brought to observe the path of rectitude, if the goading hand of severity was held over him with sternness, and a proper line of conduct prescribed for him to walk by."

Jennings goes on to call the problem, "the great curse to society and to families," and laments that alcoholics "should have so great and important trusts delivered to their charge as the bringing up, and education of children." Finally, Jennings notes, "We have done all we can for that profligate and above all the worst of boys—yet my heart often feels a tender emotion for the only child of my departed Sister, yet would I were I in circumstances that would admit make one trial more, to regain the disconsolate, the unfortunate, the abandoned S. K. Simonson. And if that will not prove effectual, if so many offers will be by him rejected, let him take his dernier resort, the enfi[l]ade of every rascal, the gallows."[17]

Another letter, written by Jennings to Mitchell twenty years later, suggests another family member had fallen to alcohol. David Jennings, Jonathan's youngest brother, had been elected to Congress from Ohio but resigned after serving only half his term. The elder brother wrote of "the wretched conduct of David, who after taking his seat as a member from Ohio has thrown himself away completely, and debased himself withal. The last I heard of him, was that he was in Baltimore, but concealed wrote to his [brother] to borrow money, but would not reveal his hiding place." Jennings spoke of being "mortified" by his brother's actions.[18]

Whatever environmental and biological advantages and demons Jennings possessed by the time he had grown into young adulthood, he now carried them on his own difficult vocational quest. Dogged by his father's strong religious convictions and a world where older siblings had already successfully established themselves, young Jonathan set out for the recently opened frontier along the southern fringe of the Ohio River valley. For a while he resided at Steubenville, Ohio, where he briefly helped his brother Obadiah in his law office, garnering important experiences as he helped his sibling in several cases before the Ohio Supreme Court. The idealistic youth was also able to observe and participate firsthand in the sometimes brutal world of frontier Ohio politics, a world not much different than he would experience in frontier Indiana. It was in Ohio, for example, that Jennings got a good look at the frontier type that one day would support him politically in Indiana. They were, in the words of one visitor, "course, large and strong, vulgar, sturdy and impudent. These vulgar Democrats" remained, according to the outsider, "attracted to liberty and understand it."[19] In short, frontier people were by nature a hard sell.

While in Ohio, a sense of vocational calling continued to elude Jonathan. Meanwhile his brother, Samuel, suggested Jonathan come to Virginia to start a career in law. "I have some intention of going to Virginia to reside as Brother [Samuel] insists very hard, and gives me great encouragement," Jennings wrote Mitchell in the summer of 1806. But that same summer Jennings reported he had "been down the river almost all summer" and found himself drawn westward to a world more open and wild than he would have known in Virginia.[20] He could not have known, as he trekked guardedly westward toward the wild Indiana Territory, that one day he would rise to the very pinnacle of political power in his future home.

2

"The place is full of rascals"

IN 1806, WHILE TRAVELING DOWN THE OHIO RIVER TO THE Indiana Territory town of Jeffersonville, the wandering Jonathan Jennings caught his first glimpse of the people he would come to live among and later serve as the state's first governor. They looked to be a particularly rugged lot. One amazed traveler, describing a group of Hoosier settlers in the Jeffersonville area at about the time of Jennings's arrival, observed several "children setting off to school; one boy came to the cabin to light his cigar, that he might take a whiff going along to school. The men smoke cigars, and many of the women (at least the married ones) pipes: we frequently saw women nursing their children with pipes in their mouths." These Hoosier frontier women were apparently a practical lot. The visitor noticed seeing them "washing on the banks of the rivers, as there is plenty of drift-wood. It saves the trouble of carrying fuel and water and it is colder on the banks of rivers than near their cabins." The children struck the traveler as one of the most unusual aspects of this new frontier: "Most of the women were surrounded by a number of young children; indeed, the first thing that strikes a traveler on the Ohio is the immense number of children, many of them almost naked, they do not appear healthy: but they look happy, rolling in the water and dirt. We often saw very little boys swimming in the river, sometimes leading others that could not walk: thus the dread of water wears off while they are very young: I never heard of any of these children being drowned."[1]

It is unclear why Jennings chose to journey alone to the Indiana Territory and start a new life among strangers in so harsh a land, especially given the fact that financially secure family members had offered to take the young man under their wings. Perhaps he felt like an outsider among his older and more successful brothers. Conversely, his rather difficult early life, on the quasi-frontier of southwest Pennsylvania, gave him insight and knowledge regarding how to live successfully in the new country, while his educational training would lend a further advantage among a mostly uneducated population. With these two assets, Jennings had the potential to be a big fish in a small pond, or so it might seem to a hopeful novice.

The most powerful drawing card for Jennings, however, was likely his desire to advance his economic status in a fresh arena. Indeed, this possibility drew many aspiring immigrants such as Jennings. One observer, witnessing the power of this new frontier to beckon even the oldest of immigrants, observed a "primitive couple" rowing down the Ohio River. The ancient couple "looked as if they might have been *pulling together* down the stream of life for half a century, without having grown tired of each other's company; for while their oars preserved a regular cadence, they were chatting sociably together, and they smiled as they invited me into their skiff." The writer noticed, "both were withered, wrinkled, and apparently decrepit: but they were sprightly and social . . . with a confidence which evinced nothing of the feebleness of indecision of old age."[2] Such stood the drawing power of the area at the time of Jennings's arrival.

It is also possible Jennings had been encouraged about the region's financial opportunities by Nathaniel Ewing, who often traveled back and forth from Jennings's Pennsylvania home to the territorial capital of Vincennes. Ewing served as assistant federal land registrar to a fellow Pennsylvanian, John Badolett. In the Vincennes region, upland southerners and would-be Virginia aristocrats dominated the social/political scene so that any new arrival, such as the twenty-two-year-old Jennings from Pennsylvania, would have been hardily welcomed by both Ewing and Badolett.

In 1806, the year of Jennings' appearance, Vincennes simmered with transition. Indeed, it bordered on the exotic in terms of diversity. Originally founded as a French trading post in 1732, the village and its inhabitants were described in colorful detail by Constatin Volney, who visited there in the summer of 1796. The houses, Volney reported, were "placed along the left bank of the Wabash, here about two hundred feet wide, and falling, when the waters are low, twenty feet below the scite of the town. The bank of the river is sloping towards the savannah, which is a few feet lower: this slope is occasioned by the periodical floods. Each house, as is customary in Canada, stands alone, and is surrounded by a court and garden, fenced with poles."[3]

After more Americans began to settle in the area, tensions arose as Anglo-Americans concocted ways to trick the original French settlers out of their land. Volney himself reported how the French felt about the practice at the time of his visit: "They complain that they were cheated and robbed, and, especially that their rights were continually violated by the courts, in which two judges only out of five were Frenchmen, who knew little of the laws or language of the English." Part of the problem stemmed from the lack of education among the French-speaking people. "Their ignorance, indeed, was profound," noted Volney. "Nobody ever opened a school among them, till it was done by . . . [a] well educated, and liberal minded missionary, banished hither by the French Revolution. Out of nine of the French, scarcely six could read or write, whereas nine-tenths of the Americans, or emigrants from the east, could do both."[4]

Conversely, most Americans living in Vincennes had little sympathy for the French, telling Volney they "had only themselves to blame for all of the hardships they complained of . . . They know nothing at all of civil or domestic affairs: their women neither sow, nor spin, nor make butter, but pass their time in gossiping and tattle, while all at home is dirt and disorder. The men take to nothing but hunting, fishing, roaming in the woods, and loitering in the sun. They do not lay up, as we do, for winter, or provide for a rainy day. They cannot cure pork or venison, make sour crout or spruce beer, or distil spirits from apples or rye, all needful arts to the farmer. If they trade, they try to exorbitant charges to make much out of a little; for *little* is generally their *all*, and what they get they throw away upon the Indian girls, in toys and baubles. Their time is wasted too in trifling stories of their insignificant adventures, and journeys to town to see their friends."[5] Whether their adventures were insignificant or not, as we shall see, the French population came to play a key role in Jennings's first political victory over territorial governor William Henry Harrison.

A more hidden culture, but nevertheless a powerful and potentially dangerous one, still persisted in the area as well. Native American tribes roamed the region in great numbers. Volney, mystified by their exotic ways, told of his first encounter with these people: "Bodies almost naked, tanned by the sun and air, shining with grease and soot;

19

head uncovered; hair coarse, black, and straight; a face smeared with red, blue, and black paint, in patches of all forms and sizes; one nostril bored to admit a ring of silver or copper; ear-rings with three rows of drops, down to the shoulders, and passing through holes that would admit a finger." On sacred occasions, or for war, Volney noted, "their hair is braided with flowers, feathers, or bones. The warriors have their wrists adorned with broad metal rings, like our dog collars, and a circle round their heads, of buckles or beads."[6]

By the time of Jennings' arrival, Indian tribes in the region often came into conflict with the ever-increasing numbers of white settlers. In one disturbing instance, Harrison was moved to complain to the secretary of war, noting how the "tribes form a body of the greatest Scoundrels in the world—they are dayly in this town in considerable numbers and are frequently intoxicated to the number of thirty or forty at once—they then commit the greatest disorders—drawing their knives and stabing everyone they meet with—breaking open the Houses of the Citizens killing their Hogs and cattle and breaking down their fences."[7] A few years earlier, Volney had also noted the corrupting power of the alcohol that was traded to the Indians by whites: "They will hold the cup with both hands, like monkies, burst into unmeaning laughter, and gargle their beloved cup, to enjoy the taste of it the longer; hand about the liquor with clamorous invitations, bawl aloud at each other, though close together, seize their wives, and pour the liquor down their throats, and, in short, display all the freaks of vulgar drunkenness."[8]

Settlements in the outer areas, those within one or two days' ride of Vincennes, stood as particularly vulnerable to Indian attacks. In one instance, shortly after Jennings's arrival, Harrison hurriedly wrote the head of the local Rangers, William Hargrove, explaining to him how he wanted one new log fort to be built in a nearby community. The correspondence suggests the level of tension and danger existing at that time: "In making the building be sure that it is strongly put together, made out of large logs and that a stockade ten feet high be built that will enclose one acre of ground." Harrison added, "The times are very unsettled. The Indians are continually grumbling because the white people are in this country and threatening that unless their lands are restored they will drive them [whites] back across the Ohio river."[9]

Jennings himself faced a host of potential dangers and discomforts upon his arrival at the remote territorial capital in 1806. Accommodations were greatly limited, as can be seen in the report of one traveler in the region. The visitor detailed how he fared at one nearby inn, "supp[ing] on pumpkins, cabbages, rye coffee without sugar, bones of venison, salted pickles, etc.—all in the midst of crying children, dirt, filth and misery."[10] Another traveler in the area noted the terrible conditions of what passed for roads, complaining that they were "almost impassable, even on horseback."[11] Bad drinking water loomed as yet another danger to newcomers. Thomas Scattergood Teas reported, for example, that he had "never known what it was to suffer for water till I took this journey—the only water I could get was from waggon ruts which the rain had filled, and as it had not rained for several weeks, they were mostly dry. This water, where it was exposed to the sun, was generally covered with a green scum, and where it was shaded, was full of musquitoes—but necessity compelled me to drink it."[12]

Hordes of stinging insects also plagued travelers and locals alike in the Wabash valley, often making sleeping at night in certain seasons all but impossible. Teas told of an encounter he had with some of the more prominent pests found in the region: "After passing the principal part of the night in continual warfare with myriads of fleas, I was compelled to retreat from the field, or rather bed of battle, about two hours before daybreak, and got a little sleep in a chair. . . . The musquitoes and gnats are as numerous here as along the sea shore, and are very troublesome." Later, Teas reported, "sitting in the smoke of a fire which I kindled, made out to keep off the musquitoes at the risk of suffocation."[13]

Along with the threat of Indian attacks, poor accommodations, poor roads, bad water, and pesky insects, Jennings also came to a region where the local white population was said by outside visitors to be especially uncouth and dirty. William Faux, an English traveler, noted in his journal how he observed "nothing between Vincennes and Princeton, a ride of forty miles, but miserable log holes, and a mean ville of eight or ten huts or cabins, sad neglected farms, and indolent, dirty, sickly, wild-looking inhabitants." Faux then complained, "Soap is no where seen or found in any of the taverns. . . . Hence dirty hands, heads, and faces everywhere. Here is nothing clean but wild beasts and birds, nothing industrious generally, except pigs, which are so of necessity."[14] Another

IHS, P130

A view of Fort Harrison near Vincennes.

23

English visitor to the region described the typical living arrangement of frontier people as "a pig-enclosure of logs, a stable of the same, open to all the winds and to the poultry, and if his log house will keep out the worst of the weather it is sufficient: and thus, with such buildings, with just as much corn and fother as will keep him, his family, and his stock, the settler passes his indolent days; smoking under the shed of his habitation."[15] Jennings would have found housing in Vincennes to be of poor quality and very expensive. One resident there, for example, wrote back East complaining, "The high price of house rents, commonly a symptom of prosperity is here a sign of wretchedness. For a small uncomfortable room hired for my office I had to pay 36 doll. a year, with the prospect of either being without fire, or of being at an additional expense of 50 dol. for a stove."[16]

Morris Birkbeck, an Englishman who often visited in the area and later settled just west of Vincennes, noted another dangerous reality found in the area: the region's tendency to draw a particularly rough and violent type of frontiersman. Birkbeck pointed out that "an unsettled country, lying contiguous to one that is settled, is always a place of retreat for rude and even abandoned characters . . . and such, no doubt, had taken up their unfixed abode in Indiana."[17] Faux believed that legal means could not restrain the rougher elements of the southern frontier population, whom he labeled "Rowdey," and it routinely proved "necessary to shew or threaten them with a pistol."[18]

New settlers from the East also could not have been prepared for the prevalence or intensity of personal confrontations on the Hoosier frontier. Faux, for example, told of seeing "a man this day with his face sadly disfigured. He had lost his nose, bitten off close down to its root in a fight with a nose-loving neighbour."[19] Another visitor to the area described one particularly brutal fighting technique popular among frontiersmen. "[They] immediately seize each other," he wrote in amazement, "and fall and twist each other's thumbs or fingers into the eye and push it from the socket till it falls on the cheeks."[20] This brutal, no-holds-barred form of fighting—often referred to by upland southerners as "rough and tumble"—had its origins on the early southern upland frontier. The rough-and-tumble style found a richly supportive environment along the Wabash River. Boatmen on the Wabash were deemed especially coarse and dangerous by one visitor, who described them as "a rough set of men, much given to drinking whiskey, fighting, and gouging, that is, they fight up and down, trying to put out each others eyes with their fingers and thumbs, and sometimes biting off each others noses or ears. A man, who resides near me, had the top of his nose bitten off, in one of these brutal frays, some years since. This is their common manner of fighting." A tenderfoot in such a rugged environment faced a menacing situation indeed if he was unfortunate enough to encounter the wrong crowd. One naive English visitor to the American frontier told of a harrowing experience when he innocently asked if it was really possible to gouge a man's eye out as easily as he had heard. A brawny frontiersman, "rose, and, walking round the end of the table, came toward me. He . . . laid hold of the hair by the side of my head, and twisting his fingers well in it, brought his thumb to the corner of my eye, against which he pressed with a force . . . that satisfied me of the possibility of removing an eye from the socket in this manner."[21]

Dueling, however, was the preferred form of settling a disagreement among the more sophisticated men of Vincennes. Fortunately, Jennings, because of his own early experiences growing up on the frontier in southwest Pennsylvania, understood the frontier mentality better than most nonsouthern migrants. He understood one could not back down from a challenge and still hope to have any influence with the majority of the population. Shortly after arriving at the untamed capital, Jennings faced his own moment of truth after he challenged a local politician to a duel. The fight never took place, but Jennings established that he could hold his own among the rugged citizenry.

The most immediate danger for a new arrival in Vincennes involved the many diseases found on the frontier and the lack of adequate medicine and trained doctors to deal with these afflictions. Perhaps the most deadly was cholera. Harrison himself often complained in letters of recurring illnesses such as the annoying ague, a common name for malaria. This affliction, which brought fever, extreme chills, and intense aching, was so common that frontier inhabitants regarded it in much the same way modern people regard the common cold. Work schedules, court dockets, and other events were adjusted to adapt for sufferers' recurring attacks. The symptoms, reported one observer, included "cold sensations which increased until the victim's teeth chattered in his jaws and he 'felt like a harp with a thousand strings.' After an hour or so warmth returned, then came raging heat with racking head pains and aching back. The spell ended with copious sweating and a return to normality."[22]

A woman who witnessed the disease striking all around her reported, "I believe this frightful complaint is not immediately dangerous; but I never can believe that the violent and sudden prostration of strength, the dreadfully convulsive movements which distort the limbs, the livid hue that spreads itself over the complexion, can take place without shaking the seat of health and life."[23] Harrison recounted a bout of the fever in a letter to James Findlay in 1801, disclosing, "I have had the ague and fever—that is, I had three fits of it."[24] A woman living in Vincennes with her husband, who served at the local army barracks, wrote her mother back in New England, telling of her bout with the annoying illness: "I find this fever Ague, a tedious painful disease, have lost flesh, they gave me some medicene to vomit me, mixed in a *pint bowl*, I put it by my bed side, & did not find it necessary to tast it, for the sight & smell had the desired effect."[25]

Another health issue common to the Vincennes area was the lack of qualified doctors and medical care, which made the contracting of any illness life threatening. Generally, doctors on the frontier lost more patients than they saved. Faux told of seeing "a poor Englishman, who some time since broke his leg, which from want of skill in the doctor, was not properly set; he is therefore now a cripple for life. This is an evil to which all are exposed. Many are now dying at Evansville [Indiana] of a bilious disorder; the doctor employed has lost nearly all who applied."[26] Jennings, himself the son of two trained physicians, endured a number of bouts of ailments in Vincennes. He often complained of the lack of qualified doctors, noting in one letter to his brother-in-law David Mitchell how one nearby county was "without a Physician except a miserable Quack."[27]

Part of the problem, as Jennings noted, involved the poor treatment given by physicians at this time. Purging, hot plasters, bleeding, and the use of mercury-laced calomel were most typically prescribed for any and all complaints. Badollet, who would later take Jennings under his wing, witnessed his own son suffer such poor medical treatment. As Badollet discovered, the cure was often worse than the illness. Writing back to Pennsylvania, Badollet related, "My son Albert whom I took with me, was very nigh falling a prey to an acute or continual inflammatory fever, which 4 repeated bleedings could hardly check, he is well now but a mere skeleton."[28] In another instance, a frontier woman told of the results of her own "over medication" of calomel: "I am just recovering from a serious indisposition which is not uncommon in this western country—having taken too much calomel or caught cold with it, or something, I was *salivated* to the most dreadful degree."[29]

Many health problems on the Indiana frontier, while not life threatening, still created great discomfort. Faux described a horrible rash that almost all new settlers to Indiana encountered: "New settlers in this state, men, women, and children, seem all exposed to an eruption, ten times worse than the itch, inasmuch as it itches more, runs all over the body, crusting and festering the hands and other parts, and is not to be cured by the common treatment for the itch, which has been tried without effect, and one instance has been known, where the sulphur and grease killed the patient by obstructing perspiration, and driving in the eruption. The doctors know of no remedy, and suffer it to take its tedious course."[30]

More destructive diseases also stalked the region, including cholera and typhoid. Vincennes stood as especially vulnerable to epidemic outbreaks, as it saw a constant

stream of people coming and going. The major problem for
the territorial capital regarding disease, however, involved
a lack of understanding about community sanitation; residents typically discarded their garbage and sewage into the
street for roaming pigs and dogs to consume. But an even
more dangerous practice had been established there, as
well. The *Vincennes Western Sun* carried a lengthy complaint about the problem during Jennings's short stay in
Vincennes. "It is not uncommon to see carcasses of horses,
dogs, hogs, etc. lying in the streets and on the common
near the village," the newspaper reported. "This is not only
highly offensive, but it is very injurious to the health of the
inhabitants. But a short time since, the dead body of a
horse was drawn from the stable into the principal street
of the town and there left to be devoured by hogs and dogs.
. . . People complain of ill health and yet they will suffer
horses, dogs, and what not, to rot at their doors!"[31]

Jennings's earlier experiences on the Pennsylvania
frontier had prepared him better than some for the rugged,
bleak environment he now faced in Indiana's territorial
capital. Indeed, the aspiring traveler had much to look forward to in terms of possibilities. While not exactly attractive, Jennings still possessed a number of positive physical
traits that would have been helpful to any aspirations he
had when he first came to Vincennes. His penetrating eyes
were blue and his complexion fair. The slim, sandy-headed
Pennsylvanian stood five-foot-eight-and-one-half-inches

tall. An early biographer also described Jennings as apparently "a man of polished manners" who was "always gentle and kind to those around him." While not a particularly good speaker, Jennings "could tell what he knew in a pleasing way." He wrote especially well compared to other writers on the Hoosier frontier.[32]

Despite the hardships and discomforts around him, Jennings's first description of Vincennes in a letter back to Pennsylvania came across as positive and exotic. To Mitchell he reported:

> Some description of this place, with its manners and customs, would fill an Octavo volume. The situation is highly picturesque, situated on the East side of the Wabash almost surrounded by a beautiful Prairie, nearly one mile wide, and about three in length, on the East of, and adjoining the Prairie, are what is called the barrens which are generally covered with shrubs five or six feet in height, and which barrens are ten or fifteen feet generally higher than the Prairie. Just on the borders of the Prairie where it adjoins the barrens, are three Sugar loaves, or curious mounds regularly formed; they are from twenty to thirty feet above the level of the Prairie and of gentle ascent from the East. From the summit of which you have a prospect of animate and inanimate nature for several miles. From their summit you can behold numerous herds of Cattle, some on account of their distance appear not larger than yearlings. You may behold at one and the same

time a hundred plows going, under one inclosure, which belongs to the French, who cultivate in Common.[33]

Jennings viewed the French settlers at Vincennes as a lazy people whose "Customs are often very ridiculous and grating to the feelings of an American."[34] One experience of Jennings with a French resident, however, proved to be captivating. Historian John A. Jakle has argued that the subject of sex rarely emerges in either travel journals or personal letters written from the Old Northwest. Nevertheless, "prostitution was everywhere," Jakle asserts, "but only an unusual event brought it out."[35] Jennings wrote Mitchell of just such an event: "As soon as I had learned French enough to speak a sentence or two to the girls—upon a short acquaintance, one of the French ladies, by no means disreputable, when an opportunity offered, thrust her hand into my crotch and handled my _____ in a very familiar way."[36] Another incident that captured his youthful interest involved the marriage of a much older French man to a young girl. The French community, Jennings reported, "convened around the house of the new couple, with bells, death's heads, and a coffin, singing blackguard verses, and ringing cow bells, striking on old kettles, playing on horse fiddles, night after night, until they got hold of him, they then put two large bells on him, one hanging behind and the other before and marched him two or three hours around town, so ended the farce."[37]

Jennings would have also witnessed political intrigue swirling all around him in the territorial capital. It is fair to suppose that Jennings found the political maneuvering exciting, at least in the beginning. Such goings on, and the players involved, captured the interest of almost everyone. Although successful frontier Indiana politicians may have been held in high esteem by the general population, they were often described as less than regal by visitors. A few years after Jennings's sojourn in Vincennes, a New York native described one local prominent politician as "poorly clad—summer pantaloons [in winter], shoddy clothes & a cloak to hide all." The visitor also made fun of the local county clerk who was a "Major-General of Militia, tavern keeper, schoolmaster, surveyor, doctor, & singing master."[38] Harrison himself cut an especially fine figure in that culture, as one woman described him, just as he prepared to go on a military campaign: "He had on what they call a hunting Shirt, made of calico & trimed with fringe & the fashion of it resembled a woman Short gown, only the ends were pointed instead of square & tied in a hard knot to keep it snug around him, on his head he wore a round beaver hat ornamented with a large Ostrich feather." She went on to describe Harrison as "very tall & slender with sallow complexion, & dark eyes."[39]

What eventually grew as most distressing to the political apprentice Jennings was the social/political hierarchy that existed in the territorial capital—the top echelon of which he could not seem to break into. Historian Gayle Thornbrough described the social levels Jennings witnessed:

> On the top rungs were the Governor and other public officials and professional men, traders, and merchants of some means, all generally young, educated, and on-the-make. At the bottom were the French, remnants of the first white settlers, poor and uneducated and an element of poor, ignorant, indolent ruffian Americans. In between were American farmers and shopkeepers. And finally there were the Indians, the few who frequented the town to trade, and the tribes who lived up the Wabash and in Illinois who offered opportunities for trade, but at the same time constituted obstacles to settlement and a threat to peace.[40]

Badollet perceived the more common farming folk in the region as "the same kind of people, whom we find in other new settled parts of the United [States], with this difference that the majority of them coming from the souther[n] States do not exhibit such habits of activity, such enterprising dispositions as their more northern neighbors." Badolett concluded his observations by asserting that the French population, "though poor and ignorant beyond conception, still exhibit something mild in their manners, whereas the Americans when placed under the same circumstances of ignorance and poverty, shew more sense or perhaps cunning attended with a savageness of manners truly repelling."[41]

As Thornbrough noted, above this cauldron of scrambling groups towered Harrison, who, along with a small band of followers soon to be dubbed the "Virginia aristocrats," maintained an almost tyrannical level of power through cunning political maneuvering. It would be this political intrigue that led Jennings early on to lament that while his prospects in Vincennes met his expectations, he nevertheless noted that "the place is full of rascals."[42] Jennings would not leave Vincennes before he learned some hard lessons about politics from the shrewd Harrison.

3

"Mr. Harrison is a man of some merit"

OPPORTUNITIES FOR WEALTH AND POLITICAL POWER EMERGED as two of the most important features in the arena where Jonathan Jennings and his political foes came to engage. Jennings himself traveled to the Ohio and Wabash river valleys in 1806, substantially after the initial political kingdom building had already taken place. At the very top of the political hierarchy at Vincennes was territorial governor William Henry Harrison. How Jennings came to challenge Harrison and, to some degree, defeat this powerful Virginia aristocrat stands as his first major political accomplishment. To understand this important event in Jennings's early career, Harrison's own rise to political prominence must be examined in order to see how the process of political engagement and kingdom building in the Indiana Territory operated at that time.

Ironically, Harrison almost did not take the position of governor when the Indiana Territory came into being in

1800. A week after President John Adams approved the act dividing the Northwest Territory, Harrison received the appointment as the executive of the newly created territory of Indiana. In those few days before the official word came, however, Harrison strongly considered not accepting the position. His work as a territorial representative had already gained him positive notice in Congress, especially among Federalist Party officials. One important leader, C. S. Wau, wrote to another party member noting, "W. H. Harrison . . . has come forward very handsomely." The writer went on to observe that the up-and-coming Harrison was certainly "as respectable a figure on the floor of Congress as any member there."[1] When Harrison received the call to go to frontier Indiana, he faced two difficult situations. The region lay at the fringe of national politics, and taking the job of territorial governor might very well take Harrison completely out of the national public view. Another shortcoming of the appointment concerned the diminished political arena the job offered. Only 5,500 settlers lived in the enormous geographic area of the Indiana Territory, leaving any newly appointed governor, politically speaking, a big fish in a very small pond. The shrewd Harrison, very much aware of these shortcomings, wrote Thomas Worthington in May of 1800 declaring, "I do not know who will be the Govr of the lower Territory—I could have it but *I will not accept it*."[2]

Two months later Harrison had changed his mind, writing Worthington, "Nothing I assure you was more distant from my intentions than to accept of the appointment of Governor of the Indiana Territory on the morning of the day on which the appointment was made but I was assailed by my friends with arguments which if not sufficient to remove all my scruples were nevertheless sufficiently weighty to make me abandon my first determination." With some pride, the Virginia native added, "It was suggested to me that as I was better acquainted than any other person so it would be more easy for me to make them Happy and satisfied with their government than a perfect stranger." After some calculation, Harrison came to the conclusion, "I thought it best not to decline the appointment but by accepting it to give myself time to look about me & take the advice of my friends."[3]

The appointment also brought Harrison a decent income that, the governor later wrote, he hoped would enable him to establish a small fund for the education of his children. Harrison's initial salary stood at two thousand dollars a year, a fairly large sum in those days, especially on the frontier.[4] The new governor quickly moved, as most settlers did, to take advantage of buying, then selling, available government land. However, Harrison, as well as many political officeholders, often had major advantages in land dealings. His heavy involvement in selling both land and preemptive rights is captured in a letter from

John Johnson to Harrison in 1806. "I went to Cincinnati," wrote Johnson, "in December last and purchased two sections of farm land . . . if you would inform me what you would sell the pre-emptives for now, it is probable I might dispose of two or three quarter sections now at this place."[5]

Prior to the Johnson transaction, Harrison had purchased several hundred acres on the Blue River in what would eventually become Harrison County, Indiana. Here he built a gristmill and sawmill. He also purchased land in the Vincennes area. Harrison happily reported to a friend of buying "a farm of about 300 acres joining the town which is all cleared. I am now engaged in fencing it."[6] In a letter to Worthington, Harrison further hinted at the economic and political opportunities he believed the new territory offered: "My situation here is as happy as I could have expected, the people are very orderly, and I believe are as much attached to me as any people ever were to a magistrate not chosen by themselves. The country about this place is I think the most beautiful in the world—& it now begins to flourish." All in all, Harrison told of being "much pleased with this country—nothing can exceed its beauty and fertility."[7]

In short order the new governor built the finest mansion to be found in the territory. In the summer of 1803 Harrison began the two-year project, one that he feared would "prove rather too expensive for my finances." In the same letter in which he voiced this fear, the thirty-one-year-old executive told of his continuing speculation in land: "I did not accept Mr. Shorts offer because I was informed that $1600 was not enough for my preemption Rights."[8] In another letter, Harrison lamented, "Is there no one . . . who will purchase my tract of land on Mill Creek? . . . I have 419 acres which I would sell very low."[9]

Harrison's regal new home, his continued holding of slaves along with the buying and selling of them, his intense land speculation, and his extensive purchasing clearly suggested he intended to create an aristocratic political system similar to what he had known in Virginia. Conversely, other activities demonstrated that the crafty governor maintained close contact with the common people, whom he knew would respond negatively to too many outright demonstrations of aristocratic behavior. Here Harrison put the knowledge gained from his early military service on the frontier to good use. He had observed that frontier militia and soldiers alike despised any leader who thought himself too good to associate with common soldiers. The frontiersmen, as one solider noted, commonly played all kinds of pranks upon them. Wisely, Harrison often "spen[t] half the day" with the local army personnel "making war upon the partridges, grouse and fish—the latter we take in great numbers in a seine."[10] Frontier folks took great pride in a governor who hunted and fished like one of them. Further, despite the fact he lived in a mansion he christened Grouseland (shades of his Virginia Berkeley birthplace), his successful high-profile dealings with the Indians kept the governor in a constant positive light with the more common element of the white population. His leadership of the territorial militia, one of the few forces that stood between the settlers and the Indians, also made him popular with the masses.

While the political world Harrison entered in 1800 lay at the very edge of national political action, it nevertheless afforded a calculating politician such as Harrison with a perfect environment for political kingdom building. This Harrison accomplished with great skill, despite the fact he and his followers apparently wished to create an elitist governmental and social structure similar to what they had known in Virginia, including the practice of slavery. Harrison and his followers also tended to be more supportive of elitist Federalist policy, which the majority of territorial settlers opposed. To overcome these political shortcomings, Harrison developed a keen awareness of the cultural characteristics of the region. Around Vincennes and in the "Illinois Country" of Cahokia and Kaskaskia dwelled a fair number of French who tended to support or oppose governmental policy en masse. Cunningly, Harrison gave the more important leaders of this group government appointments. The majority of settlers, however, hailed from the upland South and represented a more rugged and independent group, one that

House where Indiana's first legislature met in Vincennes.

stressed Jeffersonian Republican principles. Most stood against slavery, although a few did bring slaves with them. Thus, Harrison's primary vulnerability involved the common people's fervent support of popular republican government. The governor's absolute veto power stood as an especially offending policy in this regard, and this issue was often emphasized by Harrison's foes to diminish his popularity among the population of upland southerners. Other complaints included unjust taxation, the creation of institutions operating outside the democratic process, interfering with elections, and using his position to speculate in land.

Despite what seemed to be overwhelming differences, Harrison became popular among those he governed. His amazing ongoing success with upland southerners involved giving lip service to Republican ideas, working to enlarge available land through Indian negotiations, and protecting the settlers from the more aggressive tribes. The most successful political strategy, however, involved the employment of an extensive patronage system to gain support from the masses.

In the newly created Indiana Territory, government offices from lowest to greatest were exalted prizes. They provided a steady income via salary or fees in a world where sound currency rarely existed. Indeed, because of the shortage of sound money, coonskins and whiskey often served as payment in many frontier transactions. Furthermore, a government appointment, whether that of local postal clerk, captain in the local militia, or county coroner, brought much prestige on the raw frontier of Indiana. Most significantly, the system offered a network of alliances, ensuring that everyone, from top to bottom, would keep his place in the political hierarchy for as long as he cooperated with others. This system, which included little or no accountability regarding Harrison's recommendations or selections, created, in the words of Lew Wallace, a domain "clothed with power more nearly imperial than any ever exercised by one man in the Republic. He was authorized to adopt and publish such laws, civil and criminal, as were best adapted to the condition of the Territory; he could arbitrarily create townships and counties, and appoint civil officers, and militia officers under the grade of general. Most extaordinary of all, however, to him belonged the confirmation of an important class of land grants."[11]

Harrison's appointing powers verged on omnipotence. Except for federal officers such as territorial judges, every political position in the territory was chosen by him. Even in the case of federal positions, Harrison's opinion was influential. Thus, the selection of attorney general, treasurer, all county sheriffs, coroners, clerks and justices of the county courts, and the leaders of the territory's extensive militia rested in Harrison's hands. In 1805 President Thomas Jefferson, unaware of Harrison's Federalist leanings, actually turned over the responsibility of choosing the legislative council to Harrison, instructing him simply to reject "dishonest men . . . those called federalists . . . and land-jobbers."[12]

An insightful indication of how the appointing process worked down to the lowest levels of the frontier power structure can be found in a letter written by Benjamin Chambers to Harrison in 1803. Having been commissioned into the militia by the governor, Chambers was asked by "his excellency" to choose others in that area for militia positions and to make sure they would be loyal to the governor. Chambers reported back, "I have agreeable to your excellency's request selected such as I conceive will answer."[13] Harrison could also use his influence to try

to stop a federal appointment, especially when a particular prospect had challenged the governor. Such was the
case when Elias McNamee's name came forward to the
U.S. secretary of war as a possible candidate as a U.S.
army surgeon's mate. "I pledge myself to you Sir,"
Harrison quickly penned the secretary, "that there is not a
more unprincipled scoundrel in existence than this man."[14]
The unfortunate McNamee, a solid citizen who was an
antislavery Quaker, had recently attacked Harrison's stand
on slavery. Harrison's critical judgment kept McNamee
from receiving the position.

The territorial government itself, ruled almost totally
by the governor, existed as the most powerful entity in the
region. The governor, those who served in political offices
through his choosing, and the later legislature, most of
whom allied with Harrison, could make or break the newspapers with favoritism and direct the course of people and
trade with licenses for ferries and contracts for physical
improvements. As Wallace noted, Harrison possessed the
right to endow a few chosen men with extremely potent
influence by appointing them sheriffs, local judges, or officers in the militia. These positions further carried their
own appointees' privileges so that more than one layer of
political indebtedness developed. Even after the territorial government moved to the second stage on the path to
statehood in 1805, and the power of legislation passed
from the territorial judges under Harrison's influence to

an assembly, Harrison still wielded absolute veto power. His two veto selections in 1808 clearly demonstrated his displeasure at the possibility of losing any of his overwhelming executive powers. In one instance he vetoed a bill that would have negated his ability to appoint and remove the clerk of a court. Another bill, one which threatened his power to appoint the territorial attorney general, also met with an executive veto.

It is a testimony to Harrison's keen political abilities that he was able to secure not only the original appointment from the Federalist President Adams, but also reappointment from several non-Federalist administrations as well. Harrison accomplished this feat primarily by urging key militia leaders, whom he had originally appointed, to write strong letters of support when the time came for his reappointment. The wily Harrison constantly played the Indian threat as well. No sitting president would want the Indian problem to get out of hand during his administration. That Harrison could maneuver almost any group, even hardcore frontiersmen, to help him gain consecutive terms can be seen in his manipulation of an 1802 convention initially called to produce a petition favoring the introduction of slavery into the territory. Here a petition asking for Harrison's reappointment unexpectedly began to circulate as well.

One bitter opponent noted in disgust how Harrison, who had been placed in the governor's chair by the

Federalist Adams, skillfully worked his militia supporters, "laqueys and under strappers, who drew up the petitions in his favor, and put them in circulation" so that they might be sent to the new Republican administration. The frustrated critic further observed how the petition was orchestrated in a way to make it seem that the regal Harrison stood for and had the complete support of the common people.[15] Such criticism, however, failed to rally the masses against their governor.

Harrison's role as the government's primary agent with the Indians further assured that the governor would have another kind of patronage machine available. With calculated cunning, he passed out military and other contracts connected with treaty negotiations. His dealings with the Indians also kept Harrison's name before the settlers in a prominent way. They stayed supremely interested in any new areas of available land their shrewd governor might win through treaties. Harrison already carried a reputation as a successful Indian fighter, a mark of high distinction on the frontier. The bottom line to the political system Harrison constructed was that the governor granted certain men rank and prestige by appointing them to governmental or military offices or by giving them lucrative government contracts, and they in turn supported his decisions and used their own influence with the people to back Harrison's policies.

A few of Harrison's original selections for major territorial positions turned out to be mixed successes. His

IHS, P391

A depiction of the council held between Shawnee warrior Tecumseh and William Henry Harrison at Grouseland in Vincennes.

practice of choosing Virginians, like himself, caused opponents such as Jennings to label the Harrison group the "Virginia aristocrats." Two of Harrison's earliest appointees, however, John Rice Jones, whom the governor appointed as the territory's attorney general, and William McIntosh, who served as treasurer, eventually developed into Harrison's earliest political enemies.

Harrison seemed especially embarrassed about Jones, whom he reported to President Jefferson "is really one of the most abandoned men I ever knew. You will no doubt be surprised at this declaration when you recollect that he holds his appointment . . . by my recommendation."[16] Both Jones and McIntosh fell from Harrison's good graces over questionable land speculation. Both later bitterly accused Harrison of the same practice. On a deeper level, this falling out underscored the resentment those such as McIntosh and Jones, who had already established a political power base in the region before Harrison's appointment, came to have toward the powerful governor. Harrison's negative assessment of Jones to Jefferson represented an attempt at the "removal of Jones from his seat in the Council."[17] Such a bid demonstrated the darker side of political patronage. Harrison could, if he so wished, hold back support or even make a vigorous effort to unseat an uncooperative officeholder from his position. Accordingly, few men seeking any kind of prominence in the new territorial government dared to clash with the seemingly all-powerful executive.

Four of Harrison's most important appointments were southerners (Virginians or those with Kentucky connections): Henry Hurst, Thomas Randolph, Waller Taylor, and Benjamin Parke. Unlike McIntosh and Jones, these men came to the Indiana Territory at about the same time as Harrison and thus owed their allegiance to the governor rather than to any previously existing power structure. Parke and Hurst in particular grew to be Harrison's political point men, savagely attacking anyone who threatened "his excellency." Historian Andrew Cayton labeled Hurst "a virtual toady . . . serving as a stoolpigeon, spy, and mouthpiece" to the governor.[18]

Occasionally, however, political shrewdness was superceded by family bonds. In one instance, the usually astute Harrison recommended to Jefferson "my brother in law Mr. Coupland whose embarrassed [financial] Circumstances would [be] much relieved by such an appointment."[19] The wise Jefferson, however, selected Harrison's second choice, Parke.

Perhaps the strongest relationship Harrison had with any of his followers was with Randolph. Two years Harrison's junior, Randolph, like Harrison, was a Virginia blueblood with powerful family connections, received an appointment to the military (a position he did not accept), and was a slave owner. A graduate of William and Mary College, Randolph served one term in the Virginia legislature. When Randolph came to Vincennes, the governor immediately appointed him attorney general for the territory. The ambitious young man quickly enhanced his situation by marrying a woman who was the stepdaughter of General James Dill and the granddaughter of former Northwest Territory governor Arthur St. Clair. One historian noted that as "chaperoned as Mr. Randolph was by Governor Harrison, he at once took rank among the leading men of the Territory."[20]

Harrison's regal power did not go unchallenged. Despite the governor's skill at playing politics, strong criticism of his heavy-handed policies and calculating appointments came quickly. The list of Harrison abuses created a strong foundation for Jennings's later political ascent. McIntosh, originally appointed by Harrison as the territory's first treasurer, led the initial challenge to the governor's power. Harrison himself rarely attacked his political foes in public, leaving that task to his primary supporters, whose jobs and positions depended on him staying in office. Parke, for example, quickly went after McIntosh, declaring him in one letter to the editor of the *Vincennes Western Sun* "an arrant knave; a profligate villain; a dastardly cheat; a perfidious radical; an impertinent puppy; an absolute liar; and a mean and cowardly poltroon."[21] McIntosh, however, refused to fight back. Later, Randolph, who ran twice against Jennings in territorial congressional races, attacked McIntosh with a club. McIntosh, in defense, drew a dagger and seriously wounded Randolph.

In the far western part of the territory, in the Illinois Country, attacks against Harrison came from Isaac Darneille, who distributed a number of anti-Harrison pamphlets in 1805 under the title of *Letter of Decius*. One of Darneille's criticisms was the lack of representation for the western area. Settlers in this region often felt left out of the court of the Virginia aristocrats who ruled in far-away Vincennes. Darneille also attacked the Harrison patronage system, pointing out that a delegate to Congress such as Parke, under obvious obligation to the governor, could not fairly represent all the people of the territory, especially the western division.[22]

In another letter, Darneille labeled Parke an aristocrat who was bewildered and lost and who served in Congress only to secure his boss Harrison a second reappointment: "You have no doubt, been instructed by your friend, as to the *great object of your mission*; which is very plain to all the world who wish to know it. It will be your duty as well as you can, agreeably to your instructions, to keep the company of the members of congress, & tell them & the several ministers of state, handsome stories about Mr. Harrison, and say how popular he is in the territory, in order that he may be assured of his commission."[23] Darneille, addressing the building of the Harrison patronage system and how it worked on the local level to create an unbeatable network of support for the governor, asserted in one of his letters that Harrison "in order to form for himself the strongest party has taken care to commission a majority of the greatest fools in the Territory, many who cannot read or write, and who are thereby metamorphosed into a sett of petit tyrants."[24] The writer went on to give a specific example of how this process worked. Harrison had made, Darneille declared, "appointment of improper persons to offices to gain popularity.—There are three persons of the name of Whiteside, appointed and commissioned in the county of St. Clair. . . . This family and their connections are very numerous. And these appointments were made or promised at a time, when the governor courted popularity, & his

creatures were handing about petition for his reappointment." Darneille also claimed that "all three of these persons were indicted for horse stealing a few years ago; the
records of which, is now in the general court of the territory,
or the general court of the state of Ohio. . . . Two of these
persons have a seat on the bench of justice, because their
family furnished many subscribers to the petition of the
governor, and two command each a company of militia."[25]

Despite the allegations made by Darneille, Jones, and
McIntosh, Harrison's popularity remained unchanged.
Even Darneille conceded that "Mr. Harrison is a man of
some merit," who possessed "handsome manners and a
certain *je ne sais quois*, to acquire popularity with a certain
description of men." Further, Darneille noted his adversary had a talent for entertaining. "In conversation he is
sprightly and gay—can repeat a theatrical performance,
and mimick a blackguard as well as I ever saw in my life."[26]
Yet Harrison's power would eventually ebb.

The catalyst for the demise of Harrison's court rose
from its attempt to officially introduce slavery into the territory. Slavery had long existed as a part of the regional
scene, having been practiced by the French in both the
Illinois Country and around Vincennes. Later, many
American settlers from Virginia and the upland South also
brought slaves. Both situations clearly indicated that the
statute in the Northwest Ordinance prohibiting slavery had
never really been enforced. Indeed, before the formation

of the Indiana Territory in 1800, petitions for the legal admission of slavery frequently arrived at Congress from the Illinois Country. Harrison himself began to receive such petitions from the western edge of his domain soon after his appointment as territorial governor.

Two reasons likely caused the governor to strongly advocate the legal acceptance of slavery in the territory. Harrison himself owned and traded slaves while serving as territorial governor, and he clearly wished to recreate on the Indiana frontier the same world he had known in Virginia. Further, many others in his "Virginia Court" also owned and traded slaves. (Many of these same would-be lords also referred to their homes and properties as plantations.) In order to get around the ordinance's statute prohibiting slavery, an elaborate indentured service system was created. Court records, especially personal wills, indicated the degree of slaveholding and indentured service in the Vincennes area. For example, Hugh McGary Sr. in his will left his wife "two Negro women, Tenar and Poll, . . . to assist in Supporting my young Family."[27] Another will from the area directed, "may it be well understood that my youngest daughter Caroline Jane . . . receive over and above her divide two young Negroz Known in my family by name Charlotte and Abraham."[28] Henry Vanderburgh, a federal judge in the territory, requested his wife receive "two slaves Daniel and Peg" along with two black indentured servants.[29] Many Harrison supporters, such as Virginia-born Robert Evans, also bought and sold slaves and indentured contracts as a form of financial speculation.[30]

In 1805 the first legislature, under the control of Harrison, passed an act allowing incredibly long indentured contracts, often beyond life expectancy, to override the original restriction on slavery. In fact, the 1805 Indentured Servant Act legalized a form of slavery in the Indiana Territory. Note, for example, the case of Jacob, a sixteen-year-old black man brought into the territory from South Carolina by Eli Hawkins. His contract read in part: "Hawkins and the said Jacob . . . agreed among themselves . . . that said Jacob shall and will serve the said Eli Hawkins and his assigns for term of Ninety years from the day of the date hereof. [. . .] From and after the expiration of said term the said Jacob shall be free to all intents and purposes."[31] Jacob would have been 106 years old at the end of his service. Other contracts on record include ninety-nine-year agreements, but most commonly ran for forty to seventy years. One critic of the act wrote to a friend, explaining how the Harrison faction "passed an act permitting owners of negroes emigrating into the territory to bring them hither and keep them for a number of days, during which time the poor slave is at liberty forsooth to bind himself for a term of years (the favorite is ninety-nine years) or to be remanded to the state he was brought from and sold." The writer noted such an act "trampled on the

Ordinance of Congress, in that part of it which relates to Slavery."[32]

Harrison himself bought and sold slaves under the indenture law, as indicated by a letter he wrote in 1807 to a friend in Kentucky regarding a pending problem with selling a slave named Molly: "I am yet uninformed whether she has been emancipated in Ky. & bound for 15 years or whether you have made a contract with her former master to have her set free in 15 years—If she has not been indentured."[33] In an earlier 1806 correspondence, Harrison wrote of another arrangement where he offered to "freely take one or two negroes either male or female & get the favor of you to keep them til an opportunity of sending them occurred—it would make no difference whether they are slaves for life or only serve a term of years."[34] The aristocratic Virginian's strong support of slavery in Indiana can also be seen in a letter the governor wrote in 1803 to a U.S. senator from Ohio, Thomas Worthington, who had informed Parke, the Indiana territorial representative, that he would help him and Harrison to try and achieve all of their agendas except for the introduction of slavery to the territory. To this revelation, Harrison responded, "[Parke] informed me that you promised to aid him in every particular excepting that of the introduction of slaves. I am sorry you are so much opposed to this measure—but more so on account of the opinion you have given that the consent of the State of Ohio is necessary before we can have slaves in this Territory—You certainly did not consider this subject sufficiently or you would not have given such an opinion."[35]

While the western country and the area around Vincennes tended to support measures that aimed to bring slavery into the territory, a new population, rapidly moving into the southeast and eastern portions of the area, did not. Primarily composed of Quakers, poor upland southerners, and middle-states settlers, most of these new arrivals carried strong antislavery sentiments. As this region's population increased, it became a hotbed of anti-Harrison sentiment. For example, Clark County citizens, in response to the growing movement to legalize slavery, organized their own petition in 1807. Declaring that Harrison's heavy-handed policies were "repugnant to the inestimable principals of a Republican government," the petition further attacked the governor's stand on slavery.[36] More petitions to Congress from both sides soon followed, with each group claiming it represented a majority of citizens' sentiments regarding slavery.

The growing question of slavery eventually brought about two monumental changes: it turned many previous Harrison supporters against the governor, while further creating an issue that would allow a powerless new upstart, Jennings, to successfully enter the political arena. The former aspect can be clearly seen in John Badollet's dramatic shift of support from the Harrison to the anti-Harrison group.

Badollet came to the Indiana Territory from Pennsylvania in 1804 to serve as the federal land registrar at Vincennes. The appointment promised steady pay and a percent of fees for land sales. It also stood as one of the highest-profile jobs in the territory. Harrison likely had his own candidate in mind for the position, one who would fit snugly into the governor's patronage system, but the office came to Badollet with the help of a childhood friend, Albert Gallatin, who served as President Jefferson's secretary of the treasury. Unfortunately for Badollet, his personality often failed to fit into the rough-and-tumble world of frontier politics. One biographer described him as having "an intellectual bent, sensitive, inclined to underestimate and degrade himself, timid, fiercely honest, unbending, excitable, loyal to his friends, and unmercifully critical of those who did not adhere to the strict standards of conduct he set for himself." He was not, the biographer further noted, "an easy person to get along with."[37]

Badollet not only possessed a rigidity that made it difficult for him to play the political game, but he also intensely disliked the intrigue that often came with the political process. In a letter to his dear friend Gallatin, written two years before he came to Vincennes, Badollet penned, "Columbia fosters a good many unworthy sons. Offices sought for on account of their emoluments without regard for the qualifications they require, public bodies filled with interested men, public measures taken to answer private views & which proves that the evil is great, nobody surprised at it. I declare that I never went to an election without a painful depression of Spirits & my pride as a freeman considerably humbled."[38] Indeed, Badollet threatened, at first, to resign the Vincennes position, causing his surprised benefactor Gallatin to declare "your letter in which you expressed your indication to leave the place afflicted me."[39] Gallatin insisted that his friend endure, which Badollet eventually did.

Despite his deep dislike of politics, Badollet clearly understood the need to surround himself in Vincennes with men who supported his views. Early on, Badollet requested that Nathaniel Ewing, another Pennsylvanian, who had moved in and out of Vincennes since 1789, be made the federal land receiver. Gallatin, understanding the patronage system in general and Harrison's success in creating one in the Indiana Territory, wrote back to his friend Badollet saying, "I would like extremely to see N. Ewing appointed receiver, . . . but I cannot ask for too much in favour of Pennsylvania. I wish he could get a recommendation, not from Pennsylvania, but from Gov'r Harrison & others near Vincennes & have it directed to me."[40] Eventually Gallatin was able to pull strings in Ewing's behalf. Indeed, it is likely that Harrison, who constantly sought political alliances with important men in the national administration, wisely helped Ewing secure the job. Thus federal employees Badollet and Ewing initially came to reside, if not in, at least near, the powerful Harrison court. From this point, all the two men had to do was cooperate with the governor's agenda while reaping the benefits of their jobs.

At first the rigid Badollet seemed satisfied with placating the governor, whom he called "a man of fine & correct understanding, upright in his principles & conduct, a faithfull servant of the United States & highly entitled to confidence." In the same letter, however, the sensitive Badollet raised the issue of his own gut reaction to Harrison's regal style: "His having been a Soldier for a long time, & his eyes having a side glance that fathom you to the soul, render his company less agreeable to me, seem to repel familiarity & confidence, but it is perhaps my own fault."[41]

For his part, Harrison quickly began working Badollet and Ewing, requesting, for example, that they write a letter of support to Gallatin on behalf of one of the governor's favorites, Parke. This the two men did, writing, "Governor Harrison has written to us, wishing us to Second a recommendation he has forwarded to you in favour of Mr. Benjamin Parke of Vincennes for the purpose of getting him the appointment of Agent to defend the Interest of the United States before the Commissioners for adjusting the claims to land in upper Louisiana—Being well acquainted with Mr. Parke we do not hesitate to say that

we think him both in point of talents & integrity well qualified to discharge the duties of that office."[42]

Another sign of Badollet's initial support of the
Harrison "court" can be found in an 1805 letter to Gallatin
in which the land register reported, "Amongst the members [of the legislature] the following deserve to be taken
notice of for their enlightened views & usefullness. Col.
Chambers, son of General Chambers of our State, John
Rice Jones & Benjamin Parke, this last is elected to represent us in Congress and is a worthy man of an excellent
head and heart and of an independent mind."[43] Parke, a
powerful Harrison lieutenant, soon became a vicious and
relentless enemy of Badollet.

In 1805 Badollet still supported the governor, and as
his reward received an appointment from Harrison as the
head of the court of chancery. The land registrar's uphold-
ing of Harrison is also evident in Badollet's correspondence
to Gallatin regarding the Decius letters: "A poisonous rep-
tile, called Darneille of St. Louis, has been this long time
traducing the character of Governor Harrison before the
public in anonymous publications, for reasons best known
to himself." Badollet added, "Making every allowance for
the sallies of a man who is still young, & the foibles intici-
dent to human nature, I consider the Governor as a man of
true honour, of an unimpeachable honesty, and an excellent officer."[44] In another letter to Gallatin, Badollet noted
of Harrison follower Parke: "From Mr. Parke, our member

in Congress I have received many testimonies of kindness, any peculiar mark of attention you will be pleased to shew him, will be highly gratifying to me. Please to remember me to him."[45] In 1806 Badollet received yet another reward for his support of the governor, "a bargain with the Governor for a piece of land."[46] All of these instances clearly demonstrate that Badollet and his assistant, Ewing, cooperated smoothly with the Harrison political machine. Yet by 1807 cracks had begun to appear in this alliance.

On one level, the circumstances that separated Badollet and Ewing from the Harrison court involved petty political jealousies. Badollet spoke of this in an 1807 letter to Gallatin: "I forgot to tell you that during my absence some scurrilous publications had appeared against Ewing, but chiefly against me originating in the disappointment of some of the Candidates for the Clerkship. Those publications hurt me exceedingly and added poignancy to the pains I then suffered."[47] Badollet's rigidity in withholding pay from Benjamin Chambers further angered an important Harrison follower. Chambers had contracted to improve three major trails in the territory, but Badollet thought his work incomplete. Chambers quickly complained to the governor about the matter, hoping to apply pressure on Badollet to be more flexible in his assessments of Chambers's road-surveying work for the territory. Of the Chambers predicament, Badollet specifically complained to his friend, "If the men whom I have sent to view the roads, report them, not opened according to contract, how am I to act, I surely must continue to hold the balance of Mr. Chamber's money in my hands, but should he become surly and refuse to do over the roads and complete them, what steps is it proper for me to take?"[48]

More distressing to Badollet were Harrison's meddlesome attempts to get Badollet to let the governor choose those who would now review Chambers's work. In the political arena of give and take, Badollet should have relented. Instead he reported to Gallatin, "The Governor who is security of Chambers, had the indelicacy to point out to me some of his own friends, as proper persons for viewers, and is highly incensed against me, because I paid no attention to his suggestions, answered him, that nobody should know whom I would send."[49]

Harrison, who also greatly needed Gallatin's support, quickly wrote the secretary of the treasury as well, telling him his side of the story. First Harrison wisely began with praise. "When you did me the honor to recommend Your friend Mr. Badollett to me in a very particular manner I felt extremely gratified at the confidence which you seemed to have in my disposition to shew my respect for you whenever an occasion should offer. A very slight acquaintance with B[adollet] was sufficient to shew that the partiality of the friend had not exaggerated the Virtues of the Man & that he was really entitled to the encomiums you bestowed upon him—An intimacy and Confidence which knew no bounds as I believe on either part was the consequence & continued uninterrupted." Then Harrison, after giving several particular examples of where Badollet had failed to work with the governor and his supporters and had, in fact, begun to attack the Harrison administration, asserted, "But you who know Mr. B[adollet] so well need not be told that altho he possesses more virtues than are commonly the lot of one man—he is nevertheless extremely irritable & Pevish & altho possessed of a sound understanding he is so extremely diffident of himself & so little acquainted with the world that there is not a man on the earth more easily duped."[50]

Harrison's appraisal carried some truth. Badollet's greatest difficulty remained his lack of ability to play the political game. Harrison further claimed to Gallatin to have held back a petition signed by "at least four-fifths of the citizens" to have Badollet removed from the land registrar's office. This comment suggests Harrison's willingness to put up with the difficult Badollet if Gallatin could somehow convince the land registrar to ease up. Harrison blamed the falling-out between him and Badollet on the influence of Jones and McIntosh, two extreme enemies of the governor. Harrison also pointed out to Gallatin that his policies, despite the hostile and unfair claims of Jones and McIntosh, were still popular among the people. This, the governor bragged, could be seen in the lack of success his enemies had in trying to elect two anti-Harrison men to local offices:

"After making every possible exertion & bringing to them aid the prejudices of the people against the admission of negroes, the most successfull of their candidates got no more than ten or twelve American votes out of 350 & about 30 ignorant French."[51] One of the anti-Harrison candidates had been Badollet's brother-in-law, Dr. Elias McNamee. It is likely Harrison hoped all this information would cause Gallatin not to place too much trust in Badollet's complaints and perhaps cause the secretary to place pressure on Badollet to work with the Harrison group.

The shift on the part of Badollet and Ewing away from support for the governor proved crucial. Until these two men joined the opposition, the volatile Jones and McIntosh had been unable to do much to damage Harrison's popularity. For his own part, Harrison tried to stay out of the personal in-fighting until Badollet and Ewing began pushing the slavery issue. Indeed, it would be the slavery question that energized and expanded the scattered anti-Harrison forces and created a foundation for Jennings's later rise to power.

As noted, an energetic movement to introduce some form of slavery had existed in the territory since its founding. Badollet often voiced his disgust at the possibility. During his first year as land registrar, he wrote Gallatin that "negroe Slavery is also going to be introduced, & that circumstance alone would prove sufficient to drive me from hence."[52] A year later, Badollet reported, "the introduction of Slavery into this territory continues to be the Hobby horse of the influential men here. The members of the legislature have signed a petition to Congress praying for some reasonable modifications to the ordinance [the sixth article of the Northwest Ordinance]."[53] Badollet further elaborated on his feelings about slavery in early 1806, noting, "I will I suppose end my days here, provided the inhabitants, when arrived at the third grade of government do not admitt the odious system of slavery, on account of which they betray the greatest uneasiness, they have all brought from the Souther States their prejudices & fondness for that nefarious system, that measure would perhaps be attended with a few transitory & present advantages, but would entail on this country serious & permanent evils."[54]

Still, Badollet had not completely broken with Harrison at this juncture, for it was at this same time he concluded "a bargain with the Governor for a piece of land," and the two men worked closely together as witnesses at a land sale.[55] By December 3, 1807, however, Badollet had grown distraught over the attempts of Harrison and his followers to make slavery a reality. "The Legislature of the Territory have been every year pestering Congress with petitions for the admission of slavery into it," Badollet complained. Badollet then listed to Gallatin reasons not known to the general public why petitions calling for the admission of slavery should not be acted upon:

My office of Register has put me in possession of a fact of which few here have any knowledge, namely that almost all the emigrants from the Southern states to a man, who have purchased or do purchase land in this office are flying from the evils of slavery, to this only part of the United States, the climate of which will permitt them to cultivate the products, to the raising of which they are accustomed, without meeting the evils they so much wish to avoid. I am informed by them that a considerable population from both North & South Carolina, of whom wealthy Quakers form a great proportion, are preparing to move here (some have already arrived), that, could the apprehensions created by the petitions above alluded to, be quieted & the belief be solidly impressed, that Congress will not yield to those clamours, but perform their solemn promise of not permitting the introduction of slavery in this Territory, then the emigration from the aforesaid States would be very great and as it were unceasing. The emigration from the neighboring State of Kentucky is chiefly composed either of men who detest slavery from principles, or of such, as being in modest circumstances, & owing their bread to their *own* labour cannot well brook the haughty manners of their opulent neighbours the slave-holders. The members of our Legislature & their co-adjutors, whatever may be the source of their actions, prejudice or interest, have argued from wrong premises, namely that crowds of slave holders would flock here, raise the price of land and rapidly increase our population.[56]

In early 1808 Badollet angrily told Gallatin how the territorial legislatures had moved to enact an indenture system as a way of making slavery a certainty. "Could humanity, the principles of wise policy which shine in that part of the ordinance, and common-sense be insulted in a more outrageous manner?" Badollet asked. Most distressing, however, Badollet pointed out, "the executive [Harrison] gave his sanction to the laudable Act!!!"[57] By the summer of 1808, a clear break had occurred between the peevish land registrar and the aristocratic governor. Badollet wrote to Gallatin, "All is intrigue here." The governor had his own handpicked, proslavery man, Randolph, for the territorial legislature. Of this fact Badollet reported, "The vices of Courts are not unknown in this gubernatorial climate." But the duo of Badollet and Ewing had declared war themselves. "Ewing and I have made a stand against the deception practised upon the public in relation to Slavery," Badollet asserted in 1808.[58]

Another bit of correspondence would show, however, that these efforts would come at the price of health and reputation. "I have been near loosing Peggy by a nervous fever, I have myself & children been sick," Badollet wrote Gallatin, adding, "the demoralised state of the place, induce me to wish a change of situation. . . . I never shall be forgiven by some here for being an honest man, for having with Ewing and a few others began a plan of opposition to the introduction of Slavery." The high-strung Badollet ended this particular correspondence by observing, "All deception and intrigues! I drew the Petition against Slavery & hastily the report of the Committee of the House of Rep. on the same. His excellency had the imprudence to attack Ewing & me on the subject with the rage of a despot, we repelled the attack with becoming decency & firmness, and are hated therefor."[59]

Despite the difficult battle Badollet and Ewing had chosen, they would not fight alone. In early spring 1807, another Pennsylvanian, Jennings, arrived in Vincennes. Harrison himself apparently believed his political kingdom safe, having flippantly written to Worthington that the territory's newly elected representative to Congress, Parke, "will amuse you with an account of our Territorial politics."[60] Jennings, however, was about to dramatically alter the scene in a way Harrison would not find amusing.

4

"Had I played a double part"

IN 1806 NATHANIEL EWING, PERHAPS TIRED OF ALL THE sickness, danger, and political hassles mushrooming at the territorial capital, temporarily departed Vincennes. Apparently, he hoped to work in Vincennes at the land office for only part of the year, staying the rest of the time in Pennsylvania. His departure placed great stress upon fellow Pennsylvanian John Badollet. The latter complained of the situation in a letter to his political patron, Albert Gallatin, in July 1806: "The absence of Mr. Ewing is a serious inconveniency to me, to the public business, & no less detrimental to his reputation. I have written several times to him & I believe he contemplates coming here only in the falls." Badollet begged Gallatin "to urge [Ewing] to come [back to Vincennes], without letting him know that I have made the present request, and that I have said any thing about him."[1]

Badollet had ample cause for concern. As he nervously noted in the same letter to Gallatin, "the [land] sale will take place this autumn, we must have [someone with] a practical knowledge of the manner of keeping our books, that will require previous exercise, and his assistance will be necessary to enable me to begin right."[2] In Ewing's favor, before he departed he asked Jonathan Jennings to assist Badollet in the difficult work. It is likely this arrangement had been made back in Pennsylvania, as Ewing and Jennings knew each other fairly well at that time. Ewing, for example, had married Ann Breading, a relative of a girl Jennings had once courted and had often inquired of in correspondence with his brother-in-law, David Mitchell. Although greatly displeased with Ewing's frequent absences, the grumpy Badollet quickly developed a liking for the recently arrived Jennings, as noted in a bit of correspondence to Gallatin: "When Ewing left home with his family, he engaged a clerk for me for a year, a very estimable young man, well educated."[3] Badollet may have also developed some fatherly feelings for the intelligent twenty-two-year-old as well, since his own oldest son, in Badollet's opinion, "has home spun brains, which will never lead him in to abstruse Speculation."[4] In another example, the father noted his son's "hobby horse has too long been a mule." Badollet allowed, however, that, his son's "heart is pure, his understanding though not of a superior order, is correct."[5] Conversely, Jennings possessed skills and interests more in line with his new benefactor, Badollet. A final important feature, in Badollet's eyes, was that Jennings came from Pennsylvania.

Much has been written about the cultural influence of upland southerners on Indiana.[6] While considered hardy and independent people, upland southerners were also often appraised by outsiders as being "unenterprising" and possessing many "indolent slovenly habits."[7] For example, Badollet thought the southern settlers around Vincennes did "not exhibit such habits of activity, such enterprising dispositions as their more northern neighbors."[8] Today, Indiana is considered "the most southern of northern states."[9] Far less is known about the impact on the Hoosier State of middle-state settlers, especially those from the quasi-frontier region of southwest Pennsylvania. Geographer Peirce Lewis asserted that Pennsylvania played a particularly important role in U.S. history. The Keystone State's culture, argued Lewis, tended to make residents more open to new ideas than the people who lived in New England or the South. According to Lewis, as settlers of the state moved elsewhere, Pennsylvania's influence spilled westward in a great swath that stretched across much of the nation's middle portions.[10] Pennsylvania natives seemed to have brought to the Hoosier State solid work habits, along with a deep disdain for slavery and a firm belief in the importance of education—values that ran quite contrary to most of those who came from the upland south. Badollet strongly believed that Pennsylvania settlers would bring "productive industry" to the Indiana Territory.[11] While

Badollet was a Swiss native, his political and social base, once in America, became Pennsylvania. Indeed, Badollet often wished in his correspondence from Indiana "to see Pennsylvania once more."[12]

Because many Pennsylvanians such as Jennings often possessed a keen understanding of the frontier mentality, they served as a more effective leaven for change than did the few New England settlers attempting to influence the culture of the state. New Englanders, or Yankees, as they were often called, found themselves held in great scorn in the territory, and later in the southern part of Indiana. William Faux, for example, told of one incident near Vincennes where upland locals falsely accused an easterner of stealing and, even after his acquittal, all but beat him to death "as a warning and terror to all future coming Yankees."[13] This cultural situation, however, cut both ways. One Yankee woman in Vincennes, at about the time of Jennings's stay, complained in a letter back to her family in the East, "I expect we shall have to stay here all Winter, which will be very disagreeable to me, for I do not like the place or people much—Dear New England, I love thee better than ever."[14]

Thomas Twining, an English visitor, also noticed this important cultural dichotomy. "There exists," Twining reported just before the turn of the nineteenth century, "a hostile, or, at least an unfriendly spirit between many states composing the American Union." These regions, according to Twining, included New England, the South, and what he termed the Middle States. New Englanders were "prudent, moral, diligent; but with more industry than genius." Of the South, he noted, "they sometimes fight with muskets, and in their common affrays they gouge and commit other barbarities." The Middle States, including Pennsylvania, "seem to be a modification of the extremes."[15]

Similar to their upland southern and Virginia "aristocrat" antagonists, Jennings, Badollet, and Ewing quickly banded together to effect change and protect each others' interests. Jennings later connected with other Pennsylvania natives such as William Hendricks and John Graham as he constructed his own political machine. Badollet's loyalty to the young Pennsylvanian soon became evident. Because of a downturn in land sales, Badollet would be left to pay his new assistant's wages out of his own pocket, "whose salary," he explained to Gallatin, "in the present stagnation of the [land] sales, take besides my commission of ten per cent, a portion of my stated salary. It would be practicable to do now without him." Badollet went on to reflect, "but he came to this distance trusting to my honour."[16]

The young and ambitious Jennings soon threw himself into his new vocation, finding little time to write to his favorite correspondent, David Mitchell, back in Pennsylvania. He did manage to hurriedly scribble a letter in the early summer of 1807, explaining, "I expect a

line from you by [Nathaniel] Ewing, but none arrived. . . .
I cannot charge you with neglect, lest you retort—
Indeed, I have been so closely confined to my writing
desk, excepting a few days after my arrival, that I have
written but little else, than 'Sundries Dr', at which time
no paper could be had."[17] Despite the intensity of the
work, the new job seemed to come as a fantastic break for
Jennings, providing him with a bit of security in a place
where money was hard to come by. Further, his growing
friendship with Badollet put Jennings in a position potentially to move up the social and economic ladder. This was
especially true regarding economic advancement, for
Jennings's job in the land office provided him with information of great value concerning impending land sales.

It was apparent that Jennings had come to the territory to speculate in land and make a quick fortune, asserting to Mitchell that, "Money may be made next spring at
the publick sales, you will know, when and where they
will take place, as it will require a law of Congress therefor." Jennings also informed his brother-in-law that he
intended "exploring the Country that will first be offered
for sale." He then suggested, "should you be disposed and
it be convenient for to remit me money I will speculate
with the same for a certain part of the profits." One of
Jennings's older brothers had already promised to send
him "the amount of $1000 against the sales. If [I] had
been in possession of 500 dollars last spring without infor-

mation or personall traversing the lands, I could have made $1000 clear by this time as others have."[18]

For his part, Mitchell seemed more cautious about impulsive speculation. This was a good thing, given that Jennings's estimates would prove overoptimistic. Later correspondence from Vincennes indicates that Jennings also fantasized about other economic schemes. In one letter, for example, he asks Mitchell to explore the possibility of buying goods in Philadelphia and then selling them in southwest Pennsylvania. "I must trouble you to know of each of the merchants in Brownsville what quantity of cotton they would purchase and at what rate—likewise what it sells at in trade such as country linen, whiskey, etc.," wrote Jennings. "And at what for cash—when you know what each would purchase you can inform me what quantity might readily be disposed of, and at what rate."[19] In another letter to Mitchell, Jennings wrote, "If we should have a British war I am determined to risque all I can scrape in the world, and run a Contraband cargo to the neutral isles."[20]

Reality soon set in as Jennings's dreams of financial success were tempered by an economic downturn. Badollet complained of financial problems at this time, writing to Gallatin, "The allarms at the prospect of an english & perhaps indian war, have, as you well see by our returns, caused a Stagnation in the sales of lands & by diminishing my profits, subjected me to temporary, but somewhat serious difficulties."[21] In another letter, he despaired, "Times are hard, & bear severely upon me, a year more of tolerably brisk sales would have placed me in a situation free from incumbrance, but there is no sale & I cannot make the two ends meet together notwithstanding the strictest economy, so dear living is in this place."[22]

Despite the intense work that kept him closely confined to his desk and growing financial concerns, the young Jennings found time to play. By April 1809 Jennings had run up a charge of sixty billiard games at a popular local tavern. Here the political leaders of the day came to smoke, drink, and play billiards and cards, but most of all to talk politics. Records show Harrison owed for twenty-five games there.[23] But while Jennings seemed on top of things, problems lurked just beneath the political surface.

Jennings's previous training in law, along with his connection to Badollet, soon brought him improved status in Vincennes's rugged political arena. A year after his arrival, the political hopeful wrote to family members saying, "I have worked my way so well, that, I was very near being Clerk to the House of Representatives of the Territory." In the same letter, however, Jennings also gave the first indication of the tumultuous political intrigue and the powerful political hierarchy that eventually came near to crushing him: "I believe I might have been elected, had I played a double part, but being under promise on certain conditions not to offer; I could not reconcile it to myself to offer, and thereby wound my promise." Jennings's letter also demonstrates the intense political infighting that occurred, as would-be politicians scrambled to climb the ladder of power. "The Clerk of our General Court [Henry Hurst], views me with a jealous eye on account of his Office," said Jennings. "I fear I shall have to kill him before he will be at rest. I challenged him, he made concessions, as I wrote you, but since I have understood, has been insinuating something, I know not what to my disadvantage."[24] Jennings, while not elected as clerk to the territorial legislature, served in 1807 as assistant to the clerk of the House of Representatives and, in 1808, as assistant to both houses of the territorial government.

Jennings's arrival in Vincennes coincided with the Badollet-Ewing break with the Harrison faction. The political intrigue that so disgusted Badollet was about to touch his young assistant. In April 1807 the federal government began a gigantic land sale. The volume of buying soon overwhelmed Badollet and Jennings. The former, something of a nervous personality anyway, described the hectic event as rough and rugged locals came pouring into the land office demanding attention. "We went to work on the following day under circumstances extremely unfavorable," Badollet observed. "The first fruit of our inexperience was to have sold on that day

19 tracts, by far more than we could manage." While under this pressure to work quickly on several things, all at the same time, Badollet told of being "surrounded by a croud of purchasers, who without feelings or discretion would teaze me with their entreaties to be dispatched & by endless questions, the extreme fear of mistakes exposed me to the commission of many. That first week forms an epocha in my life which I shall ever remember."[25]

The land sales event of which Badollet wrote was a major happening in the region and, given the political posturing at Vincennes, an eventual source of many vicious rumors. Badollet grew so despondent over the distortions and lies, ensuing fights, and lawsuits that he confessed to Gallatin in early 1808, "Except Ewing I do not choose to consult any body. Very few exist here on whose Judgement or candour I would like to rely, and I am so tremblingly alive at the fear of doing wrong, that the idea of sinister views forces itself upon my mind whenever any person volunteers his opinion to me." Of the town itself, Badollet grumbled, "of all the little towns of the United States, I do not believe there is another one, which contains so much selfishness, such disregard of principles, & where judgement is more warped by interest."[26]

The bickering rapidly accelerated to a much higher level when Henry Hurst, clerk of the general court and well-known Harrison supporter, brought charges of fraud and wrongdoing against the Vincennes Land Office, cit-

ing Ewing in particular. The portly Hurst often played the
henchman role and, as the ultimate reward for his loyalty
over the years to Harrison, would be granted the privilege
of riding his horse on the right side of Harrison at his
presidential inaugural in 1840. Ewing and Waller Taylor
had speculated on land, profiting as much as $4,900,
according to the Hurst complaint. Ewing soon brought
a countersuit against Hurst for slander, leading to a
physical confrontation between the two men. Badollet
reported to Gallatin the horrible results of the feud: "For
some previous falsehoods spread by H. Hurst, Ewing has
brought suit against him, in consequence of which he has
had notwithstanding his efforts to avoid it, a scuffle with
him [Hurst], in which our friend has been stabbed in four
or five places. He owes his life to the smallness of the
instrument, which could not penetrate deep enough to
reach any vital part."[27] As noted previously, Jennings himself had already backed down Hurst by threatening to
duel with him. The tension between the two men grew,
however, as Hurst expanded his attacks against Badollet
and Ewing to include land office staff members. Jennings
soon discovered that he had made a profound and determined enemy.

Badollet told the Pennsylvanians' side of the story
regarding the land speculation charges in a letter to
Gallatin in October of 1807: "Mr. Hurst has become the
mouth piece of the party in an open manner: he has ever

since the sales spread the most atrocious calumnies against Ewing, who is by him more particularly marked for destruction."[28] Eventually, Gallatin gave his friend a pep talk, as well as advice on how to endure the endless fighting: "As to your squabbles & disappointment, they are matters of course. At what time, or in what country, did you ever hear that men assumed the privilege of being more honest than the mass of the society in which they lived, without being hated & persecuted? . . . All we can do here is to fulfill our duty without looking at the consequences so far as relates to ourselves. If the love and esteem of others or general popularity follow, so much the better. . . . When you are tired of struggling with the vice & selfishness, rest yourself, mind your own business, and fight them only when they come directly in your own way."[29]

The twenty-three-year-old Jennings was soon caught up in the political maelstrom as well. The other participants were much older and consequently much more politically savvy than Jennings. Harrison was thirty-five; Badollet, fifty; Ewing, thirty-six; Hurst, thirty-nine; Benjamin Parke, thirty-two; and Thomas Randolph, thirty-eight.

By mid-1807 men loyal to Harrison, especially Hurst, looked for ways to please "his excellency" and gain favor in the governor's court. Hurst was already working the land speculation "scandal" when another event of use came along. In mid-September Jennings wrote Mitchell telling him of his attempt to secure a position as the clerk of the House of Representatives of the Indiana Territory. Political intrigue, however, ruined Jennings's attempt. After Jennings agreed to drop out of the contest, Hurst apparently spread rumors about Jennings's being part of a political deal. The slippery Hurst probably objected to the political currency Jennings might receive for stepping down. In the same letter, Jennings observed that Hurst had grown madly jealous of his rise to prominence. With chilling certainty, Jennings added that he was prepared to kill his rival.[30]

The deal which so enraged Hurst also involved Jennings's opponent for the clerk's position, Davis Floyd. The tall, powerfully built Floyd was known for his courage and his love of living on the edge. The latter characteristic likely got him involved with Aaron Burr and what came to be known as the Burr conspiracy. The event, in 1807, involved Burr's attempt to detach the western states and the Louisiana Territory from the union. Several men who would later become prominent Hoosier leaders were involved, to a greater or lesser degree, in the plot. Captured by federal officials in the Indiana Territory in 1807, Floyd was indicted in the territory that same year for his participation in the Burr scheme. The trial, however, ended up as something of a farce. Floyd was fined ten dollars and three hours in jail by two sympathetic judges. Waller Taylor wrote President Thomas Jefferson, explaining that Floyd "had been convinced that the [Burr] expedition had the approval of the government." The judge also noted that the territory "had no jail in which to secure Floyd, and that a heavier fine would work a real hardship on his family."[31]

Three days after Floyd's conviction, sympathetic friends in the legislature, mostly from the eastern part of the territory where the greatest anti-Harrison element resided, selected the dark-haired Floyd as clerk of the House of Representatives. Floyd stood firmly against slavery, as did many others in the eastern portion of the territory. In that respect he opposed Harrison. Jennings's dropping out of the race had guaranteed the antislavery and anti-Harrison Floyd would win the position. Floyd's election was a slap in the governor's face, and it was likely Hurst's knowledge of Jennings's role in the victory that so angered the Harrison loyalist. A great squabble soon ensued over Floyd's election as clerk. General Washington Johnston, a local political leader who had staunchly opposed Harrison in 1805 on the issue of slavery in the territory, and Luke Decker, another early political leader, quickly defended the selection of Floyd in a pamphlet Jennings came to certify. The *Vincennes Western Sun*, a strong supporter of the governor, criticized Jennings for doing so. For his part, Harrison, angry over the House's choice, hurriedly revoked Floyd's commission as a major in the Clark County militia and as pilot at the Falls of the

Ohio. Things, however, were about to grow even worse for the political novice Jennings.

Vincennes University had been founded in 1806. The school represented the expansion of public education called for in the Northwest Ordinance. The territorial legislature approved a classical course of study for the university, including literature, science, law, medicine, mathematics, and theology. Like everything else in the territorial capital, the institution's board of trustees was not immune to politics. Membership embraced both Harrison and anti-Harrison men, including Harrison himself, along with Badollet, Ewing, Hurst, and others. During one especially hot meeting in August 1807, Johnston, the clerk of the board, resigned. Selection of a clerk pro tem quickly kindled the conflict between pro-Harrison and anti-Harrison blocs. With the support of Badollet and Ewing, the anti-Harrison faction emerged victorious, selecting Jennings for the position by a seven to five vote over Hurst. Harrison, livid at the defeat of his most loyal backer, tendered his resignation from the board before the meeting was over. At the next board meeting, Jennings found himself chosen as the permanent clerk. By September Harrison had second thoughts about giving up his influence on the board. He was easily reelected to the board and again selected to be its president by his supporters, thus keeping alive the feuding atmosphere at the board meetings.[32]

Johnston, who served as Vincennes's first postmaster, had trekked to the frontier town seven years before Harrison. Johnston spoke French fluently, had married a local French woman, and was a great advocate for French rights. One local described him as "very fond of dancing and a constant attendant to all the French balls." Physically, Johnston stood less than five feet tall and possessed "very black eyes, hair, and whiskers." With "a full round face, small hands and feet," the diminutive politician offered an affecting presence, as he often "wore black cloth clothes, and a high crown hat."[33] As fate would have it, this petite but fiery man's actions were about to change Jennings's life forever.

The university board coveted the large area in Vincennes that served the original French settlers as a commons. The board eventually drew up a petition to Congress asking that the land be taken away from the locals and given to the school. In August 1807 Johnston addressed a protest meeting of the French inhabitants of Vincennes and was instructed in a resolution from that meeting to oppose the university's acquiring control of the land, which had been assigned by earlier territorial law to the local French population.[34] Johnston carried out his mission by putting up a vocal fight about the plan at the August 29, 1807, meeting of the board, causing the request for the commons to be dropped from the panel's petition to Congress.[35] Still, the infighting did

much damage, and Johnston ultimately handed in his resignation. In a letter to the *Vincennes Western Sun*, published April 20, 1808, and signed "Sand and Rosin,"
Johnston's departure from the board, an event that led to
Jennings's selection as the new clerk, was said to have
been a direct result of the board's attempt to gain control
of the commons.[36] Johnston further stoked the flames by
hurriedly writing a statement explaining how the
Harrison-dominated board had tried to take the land
away from the local French inhabitants. Needing support
that his story was true, Johnston asked Jennings to certify
the account. Jennings made the mistake of doing so without the board's knowledge. The pro-Harrison forces had
been waiting for such an opportunity.

At its April 4, 1808, meeting, the university's board
formed a committee "to enquire into the conduct of
Jonathan Jennings as Clerk of the Board." On November
21, 1808, "the resignation of Jonathan Jennings as Clerk
of the Board was received and read."[37] The *Western Sun*
noted that it was Jennings "who certified the proceedings
of the Board of Trustees for the Vincennes University,
without the consent or the knowledge of the board." A
letter to the *Western Sun* on April 20, 1808, signed "Sand
and Rosin," stated that Jennings "certified the Board of
Trustees' proceedings in connection with its attempt to
gain control of the Vincennes Commons and that the cer-
tification had been requested by General Washington

Johnston."[38] Johnston's attempt to take responsibility and thus protect the young Jennings from attack failed. Opponents smelled blood and were determined to drive Jennings from the political field.

On a deeper level, Jennings was attacked because of his friendship with Badollet and Ewing, who constantly fought to keep the "G'r and his sycophants [in] the Board of Trustees," from misusing the land fund that was meant to support the school. If not protected, Badollet had explained to Gallatin, "the depositories of a sacred fund would have been consumed for the benefit of their [the Harrison faction's] own families and a few Gentlemen of Vincennes."[39] Harrison quickly wrote Gallatin to give his side of the story. He called the university episode "a trifling misunderstanding."[40] Trifling or not, by the time Jennings's letter of resignation was read in November 1808, he had already fled Vincennes.

Toward the end of his perplexing sojourn, Jennings wrote his sister, Ann Mitchell, expressing the growing loneliness he faced in the hypercompetitive territorial capital. At the heart of his complaint lay his growing need for companionship. "To me your letters [are] too short on many accounts," he told his sister. "You never inform me of Miss Breading, Miss Bowman. And more than that, your promise to give me information concerning Miss Mahan, has never been fulfilled."[41] Jennings also hinted that he was considering leaving Vincennes and finding a place offering more opportunities than the Harrison-dominated territorial capital provided. To Ann, he reflected, "I think that Jeffersonville [Indiana] in a year or two will be a very good place for you." Jennings also perceived that Harrison's grip on territorial politics might be waning. "It is very probable," he wrote, that Jeffersonville could shortly "be the seat of Government for a new state."[42] It would be in Jeffersonville, and then in nearby Charlestown, where Jennings would lick the political wounds suffered in his difficult and disappointing Vincennes stay and start anew. Surely Jennings was happy to be leaving Vincennes, a place his Pennsylvania friend, Badollet, asserted "exhibit[ed] a profligacy of morals not to be met with in no other part of the United States."[43]

5

"Wherever Jennings goes he draws all men to him"

NEW AND UNFAMILIAR SITUATIONS ALWAYS BROUGHT OUT Jonathan Jennings's demons, a throwback, perhaps, to the time when as a seven-year-old he lost his mother and then found himself being dragged to a new frontier home in southwest Pennsylvania. Jennings's rising anxiety in 1808 can be seen in the letters he wrote soon after he arrived in Jeffersonville, an Indiana town on the banks of the Ohio River near Louisville. The political intrigue he had endured in Vincennes seemed to have aged him beyond his twenty-four years. Furthermore, the impending death of his beloved brother, Ebenezer, did not help Jennings's mood. In a letter dated December 1808, written just two months after leaving the territorial capital, Jennings lamented to David Mitchell that his own recent financial failures paled "compared with the melancholy" news of his brother's painful last days.[1]

In the same letter, Jennings explained why he left Vincennes so abruptly. Perhaps a bit of pride kept him from mentioning the political hassles and painful defeats he had suffered there: "The summer after I went to Vincennes my attention was occupied in the Land Office; the following fall and winter I was sick and unable to attend to business of any kind which was the cause of my leaving Vincennes." More specifically, he related, "I laid out all the money I could raise upon land and was obliged to sell at a great discount in order to pay some of my debts, and my sickness and disappointments rendered me unable to meet the payments." Financially, Jennings was in desperate shape and begged Mitchell to intercede with Jennings's father for aid. "Sickness and disappointment have been the cause of my making some sacrifice in so much that I am embarrassed—otherwise I should have been up this fall to see you, but could not," said Jennings. "I am rather of opinion that I shall not be able to visit you next spring unless Papa will assist me to 50 or 60 dollars. I have to request that you will see Papa on my behalf and request him to assist me. I am in want for I know not the time I may be pushed for the money, the name of which will be an injury to me in my profession; as I am settled where I may yet be called a stranger. . . . Insist upon Papa to help me."[2]

On the positive side, Jennings had arrived in an area where the general population possessed values closer to his own. Here in the southeast and eastern portions of the territory, for example, could be found more people who opposed slavery and the aristocratic ways of Governor William Henry Harrison at Vincennes. Many of them also came from middle-state regions, such as Pennsylvania, rather than the more backward upland south. Another situation also improved Jennings's standing. Writing to Mitchell, Jennings noted, "I can assure you Sir . . . there are several characters in the County who know my father and yours in Law, and on account of which I am as well received as I could expect as my residince in Clark County only began one month since."[3]

Yet another theme which emerges in the letter is Jennings's determination to convince the Mitchells to move near him. The lonesome Jennings made his case by pointing out Jeffersonville would be the likely capital once the territory moved to statehood. (Jennings was wrong about this.) Further, Clark County was "without a Physician except a miserable Quack," a situation Jennings hoped might be attractive to his physician brother-in-law. Much of the letter celebrates the advantages of the region. "[I]t is tolerably well watered Country, soil generally rich, and level and will after a few years, afford fine roads for Carriages, and land is quite cheap," Jennings said. Then came the familiar appeal regarding his sadness due to his separation from family members. "Come on and settle or see the Country and we shall be near each other," he wrote. "It has been a long time since we had an interview, now going on three years. It is my desire and determination to be near my sister and you. . . . If you do not settle in this County s[ome] Physician will."⁴

In another letter to his sister, Jennings asserted, "Your first letter since my long absence came to hand last mail. You confess you have been negligent. You know my [o]nly Sister that I have never been unwilling to forgive any person much less yourself. I long to live near you and enjoy your society. I have been advizing the Doctor to move hether, it is a fine Country and as I informed him, I can assure you that there has never been an instance of the consumption proving fatal." Jennings still bemoaned his older brother's passing: "Brother Ebennezzer will never see me more. I would give great satisfaction to once more converse with him before he leaves the world, but I cannot." This led Jennings to continue to reflect on his own loneliness. "I am rather unhappy at such a distance from my friends and I am very anxious to see Pa & Ma," he said. "Prevail upon the Doctor to live in this Country and then I shall be contented. I will marry and we can enjoy the sweets of reciprocal friendship. Rest assured Dear Sister, that you claim and possess a place in my heart which time can never supplant until I shall go the way of all the earth." Jennings also alluded to his desire to find a mate. "I am determined to marry so soon as I can please myself," he confided in his sister. "The young ladies will look sharp when I come up to see you, or else I will come around them."⁵

Strangest of all the correspondence written during this time were the letters penned to John Graham, a man Jennings had known in Pennsylvania and befriended again in Clark County. Jennings hoped Graham would stay on or near his farm and help with its upkeep, as politics often pulled Jennings away from essential chores. In April 1809, in the midst of his first political run for office, Jennings discovered his friend had abruptly left for the Louisiana Territory. Heartbroken, Jennings wrote:

> Much was my disappointment, when I returned to this place and found you gone—gone for four years—gone without even leaving me one line to remind me of the past—the past which promised me (I thought) a lasting friendship—a friendship which I prised as being founded on the firmest basis—a basis which alone is capable of supporting real friendship, I mean the basis of an honest heart—a free and generous mind guarded by the strongest barriers of well settled principles of morality & rectitude. Graham, to you could I have deposited the greatest secrets of my heart & in your friendship I anticipated much.—I hope you will not forget me, we may see each other I fondly hope it. I could write much but Maxwell insists upon going—Believe that you[r] welfare is the most ardent wish of your friend very sincerely.[6]

Jennings ended this strange beseeching letter by explaining, "I am a Candidate for Congress & I think I shall succeed, in Clark & Harrison Counties I shall not lose 50 votes."⁷ Indeed, it was this wild and wooly campaign that took some edge off of his unhappiness. In 1809 Congress granted the Illinois portion of the region the right to separate from the Indiana Territory. It also enacted legislation that permitted the people of both territories to vote for their representatives to the territorial council and for the territorial delegate to Congress as well. These actions wrought a major turning point in Indiana politics, pitting Harrison and his court against an ever-increasing rival movement. Now, with Harrison's traditional stronghold of support, the Illinois Country, gone from the political mix, the governor stood in grave political danger. The slavery issue especially empowered the anti-Harrison faction, as evident in several pieces that appeared in the *Vincennes Western Sun* in 1809.

John Badollet's brother-in-law, Elias McNamee, energized the controversy early on when he suggested that any slave owner or supporter of the slavery system in the territory possessed Federalist leanings. Such an accusation carried an awesome punch on the frontier, where the Jeffersonian Republican philosophy was the one major political position. Claiming Federalist notions branded one an elitist, a supremely unpopular position. McNamee asserted that the introduction of slavery had better defined the two parties. Federalists clearly wanted the system, McNamee claimed. He then described Federalists as aristocrats who distrusted the people and the Jeffersonian Republicans as democrats who had faith in the people. The reader was left to easily discern that Harrison and his court plainly fit the Federalist definition. General Washington Johnston added his own anti-Harrison arguments to the mix, suggesting that the labor of the poor would be reduced in value by competition with slave labor. Supporters of the slave system soon countered. One writer argued that the slave owner could not undersell the farmer. He also asserted that slaves were dangerous in only a few states, and that their diffusion from the South would benefit the slaves as well as the southern states. Other opinions soon appeared in the *Western Sun*, some attacking Harrison's despotic actions.[8] All in all, these issues only fanned the flames created by the election for territorial representative.

The 1809 Indiana territorial election for congressional representative featured one of the biggest political upsets in the region's history. Harrison's choice for the position was one of his very favorites, Thomas Randolph, a thirty-eight-year-old Virginia native of great refinement. As Harrison's choice for attorney general for the territory, Randolph had cut a fine figure at capital social functions. The Virginian was a perfect fit in the Harrison court and seemingly a shoe-in for the representative position. Randolph's chances, however, had actually been limited to a degree by the division of the territory, which had carried the pro-slavery population of the Illinois Country out of the political equation. Furthermore, a great number of antislavery settlers were beginning to fill the eastern portion of the Indiana Territory. All they lacked was a leader around whom they might rally.

Two men quickly put their names forward as candidates for territorial representative, Randolph and John Johnson. Randolph seemed to have a lock on the position. As added insurance, Randolph quickly tried to placate both proslavery and antislavery groups whose concerns had been heightened by the growing number of handbills and newspaper articles now surfacing on the volatile issue. In an address to the public, printed in the *Western Sun*, he declared, "You already know my sentiments on this subject, they have been without disguise, expressed on all occasions . . . I would have the issue put to sleep! You say, and I believe it probably, a majority is opposed to it. I differ with them in opinion, my voice would be in favor of the introduction, let us now however, agitate this question, when more important subjects loudly demand our attention—you may stigmatize me with the odious epithet of federalist or aristocrat. Thank God the public understands better."[9] Vincennes native Johnson also attempted the same strategy of distancing himself from his previous proslavery position. Jennings, meanwhile, came into the race in an unanticipated manner.

It is difficult to understand why Jennings ran for this office. He was very young, had no political experience or voter base, and was going up against the most powerful political machine in the territory. He seemed to have no chance at all for success. But fate, a force Jennings himself so often pondered, stood as the primary player in this particular election. Although a political novice, to say the least, Jennings entered the contest at a time when destiny offered an issue that enabled the young upstart to carry out an improbable victory.

A rather imaginative version of how Jennings came to enter the political fray can be found in Indiana historian Jacob P. Dunn Jr.'s *Indiana: A Redemption from Slavery*. While probably exaggerated, it is the only version handed down. According to Dunn, several days after the election was announced, Jennings, visiting Nathaniel Ewing in Vincennes, was mounting his horse for the journey back to Clark County when Ewing said to him, "Look us up a good candidate for Congress." Jennings's reply startled his Pennsylvania friend: "Why wouldn't I do?" According to Dunn, "after a few minutes' conversation they concluded that Jennings would have a fair prospect of success in the race, if the people of the eastern counties would accept him as candidate."[10] The biggest liabilities Jennings carried were his young age and his lack of a political machine.

Though young, Jennings had grown politically cunning, thanks in part to his painful Vincennes apprenticeship. Leaving Ewing, Jennings hurriedly traveled to Charlestown in Clark County to meet an anti-Harrison group led by the Beggs brothers. Charles and James Beggs had both left Kentucky and moved to Clark County, Indiana, because of their disdain for slavery. Although only twenty-five years of age, Jennings apparently had a very mature manner about him. He rather quickly persuaded the leaders from this area to support his candidacy. If, however, Jennings hoped to beat Randolph, he had to garner even more support in the eastern portion of the state. He quickly traveled farther east to try to attain support in the Lawrenceburg district. In this effort, he ran into a brick wall. Fervent Harrison supporters General James Dill and Captain Samuel Vance held political sway in the immediate area of Lawrenceburg. Fortunately, Jennings encountered better luck in the northern portion of Dearborn County. Here a large group of Quakers had settled after leaving the South because of slavery. A number of middle-state immigrants, including those from Pennsylvania, were there as well. The area had already pledged to support an antislavery and anti-Harrison candidate, but knew little or nothing about Jennings. The baby-faced Jennings, who some called "a beardless boy," had his work cut out for him. Perhaps because of his relative sophistication, he was also labeled by Dill and other detractors as a "cold potato." Dill also joked that, if elected, Jennings would not be able to find his way to Washington, D.C.[11]

Further harming Jennings's chance at winning was Harrison's unabashed campaigning for Randolph in Knox

County. In a letter to one editor after the election, Jennings accused Harrison of writing "electioneering letters to officers of the militia and others, tending to prejudice the minds of the people against the afterwards successful candidate." Jennings also denounced the governor for publicly pledging "himself for his friend [Randolph]." Finally, Jennings asserted that "at the distance of eighty miles from the place of his residence in the Territory," Harrison did "address the voters when assembled at the Polls, in favor of his friend Mr. Thomas Randolph."[12]

Allegations of illegal land speculation while working for Badollet also haunted Jennings's campaign efforts. Still, he pressed on. As the election grew close, Jennings all but conceded Knox County and poured his energies into the eastern portion of the territory. Perhaps the most significant factor in Jennings's favor was his own frontier background in western Pennsylvania and his sudden discovery of his growing talent for public persuasion. "In personal approach to the voters, Jennings was far superior to his opponent," Dunn noted. "He knew how to bend far enough to conciliate and yet retain respect."[13]

It is Dunn, among all other earlier Hoosier historians, who related an almost mythical saga of Jennings's first political campaign. Dunn began the story of the campaign by telling of Randolph's attempts to woo the voters in the eastern portion of the territory: "It was at a log-rolling on the farm of David Reese, in Dearborn County," Dunn

wrote. "Randolph came up on horseback and was received
by Reese with the common salutation of 'Light you down.'
Randolph dismounted, and having chatted for a few minutes, was asked by Reese, 'Shall I see you to the house?'
Randolph accepted the invitation, and, after remaining
there for a short time, rode away." Randolph failed in one
important way; he did not offer to help work or play
among the frontier citizens. The next day, a boyish-looking
Jennings arrived, "who had a similar reception, but to the
invitation to repair to the house he replied, 'Send a boy up
with my horse and I'll help roll.' And help roll he did until
the work was finished; and then he threw the maul and
pitched quoits with the men, taking care to let them outdo
him though he was very strong and well skilled in the
sports and work of the frontier farmers."[14] While Dunn's
account probably verges on myth, Jennings possessed a
talent for getting along with Indiana's frontier populace.
Dill trailed Jennings, hoping to find and exploit any weak-
ness but instead finding only bad news to report to
Randolph. In one letter he lamented, "Wherever Jennings
goes he draws all men to him."[15]

One effective weapon Jennings wielded against
Randolph involved his success in connecting his foe to
Harrison and the "Virginia aristocrats." In a letter to the
Western Sun, for example, Jennings asserted, "Our territo-
rial government is exercised by a 'glorious situation,' too
nearly daily sacrificing at the shrine of ambition and

intrigue, which honest men are exhibited to public view, as objects of detestation." Throughout the campaign, letters from a number of citizens flooded the *Western Sun* office. One writer, who signed himself "A Farmer," offered an extensive narrative concerning the evils of slavery, written by Jefferson. It was, in effect, a pro-Jennings piece. Conversely, a writer calling himself "An American" bid the people of the territory to unite with the nation against international militancy and urged them to elect Randolph, a statesman whose wisdom and political skills far outshone his rival. Johnston mocked Randolph's hope that slavery could be "put to sleep." "A Voter" wrote to the *Western Sun* labeling Randolph as the candidate possessed with independent thought, rather than one who was a "political weatherneck who trembles at every breeze, and points always to the fluttering gale of popularity." The same writer brought up the old charges against Jennings regarding illegal land speculation. Accounts noting the family relationship between Randolph and Jefferson also surfaced in the *Western Sun* during the campaign. Jefferson stood as a hero to most frontier people, and some writers to the paper contended that a vote against Randolph was a vote against Jefferson. Johnston, however, stepped forth to harshly deny this notion, pointing out that Jefferson was not "a friend to slavery."[16]

Jennings's continual condemnation of the Harrison group's high-handedness, along with the slavery issue, resonated strongly with many voters. By this juncture, the Harrison faction understood their candidate faced a grow-ing challenge in the eastern section of the territory, and a kind of panic soon set in. Randolph tried to counter the accusations against him, declaring he had little connection with Harrison other than friendship and that he would not encourage slavery in the territory unless instructed to do so by his constituents. Despite Jennings's skill and deter-mination, Randolph still had a realistic chance of winning if only he could attain votes that were likely to go to the other Knox County candidate, Johnson. To counteract this problem, Randolph issued a handbill explaining that a vote for Johnson was in fact a vote for Jennings. Ultimately, Harrison himself, under the name "Detector," released a scathing political broadside. Badollet complained that the pamphlet was "withheld till the last moment, till it was too late to rebut it." The piece was "intended as a last and irrepellable blow against Jennings."[17]

In the end the anti-Harrison group's efforts to paint Randolph as an aristocrat directly under the governor's influence and slavery concerns paid off. Dearborn County gave Jennings 143 votes and Randolph 72. In the northern area of that county, every vote had been for Jennings except one. In nearby Clark County, Jennings had done even better, winning 219 votes against only 16 for Randolph. Jennings needed every vote he could obtain from the east, as in Harrison County he had won only 22 votes, compared to 83 for Randolph. Knox County voted heavily for Randolph, giving him 231 votes to 44 for Jennings and 81 for Johnson. The final tally stood: Jennings, 428; Randolph, 402; and Johnson, 81.[18]

As Randolph feared, Johnson had played the spoiler. The resulting wound between Johnson and Randolph almost led to a fierce confrontation, as a letter from the latter to Samuel Vance indicated. Randolph related how his Knox County rival "walked with a large hickory stick for some days. Informed by my friends that they had good reason to believe it was intended for me, and earnestly urged by them to place myself in a situation for defense, I thoughtlessly followed their advice, and carried also a stick for one evening and then threw it away, censuring myself for the folly of suspecting his intentions." Randolph went on to explain that the two opponents eventually made peace: "A day or two afterwards, however, the truth was discovered that his was a weapon of defense and not offense, for he apprehended an assault on him by me, for which I had no cause save his hostile appearance. Warlike appearances have vanished, and we treat each other politely in court, and touch hats as we pass on the streets."[19]

The Harrison faction was stunned by Jennings's victory, as Harrison had pushed incredibly hard for Randolph. Badollet wrote to Gallatin of the governor's intense election maneuverings, noting, among other actions, Harrison's "writing letters on the subject in every direction . . . his dispatching emissaries to every corner some mounted on his own horses to electioneer," his publishing "the praises of his dear Randolph. . . . What will you say of his leaving a parcel of Braves in Vincennes, all his intimates, who overawed the election, and by their violence so terrified the voters, that numbers of them retired without voting at all, when himself was posting to the eastern counties to intrigue amongst the people and even harangue them on the election ground?" Badollet further added that Harrison had stated publicly, "'If you want me to be your Governor again vote for Mr. Randolph, but if you wish me not to be reappointed vote for Mr. Jennings.' . . . By such and thousand other arts . . . the citizens of this county & a few of the others who had always been on our side became lukewarm or apostates and voted as they were bid."[20]

In Badollet's opinion, it was the issue of slavery that finally turned the tide for Jennings, maintaining in a letter to Gallatin that, "The question of slavery formed the touch stone [of Jennings' victory]." Badollet further elaborated, "Mr. Jennings being decided on that point & knowing besides a number of precious secrets, has therefor drawn upon himself the (honourable) hatred of our Executive & of his hirelings by whom he has been very indecently treated." It is clear, however, that Jennings's antislavery position had little to do with the practice as a moral issue and much to do with brandishing an effective political weapon against his opponents. Badollet went on to tell Gallatin of his growing fondness for the young politician, who, in all likelihood, had become like a son to the land registrar. "His conduct towards me has attached me to him & every attention you'll think fit to shew him shall be gratefully acknowledged by me," Badollet said.[21]

An embarrassed Harrison wrote to Gallatin as well, explaining his own views regarding Randolph's stunning loss. One item suggested that Jennings may have gotten some revenge for being kicked off the Vincennes University board of trustees after siding with Johnston's attempt to keep the Commons open for the French population. "In this County every exertion was made to get the French votes for Jennings the candidate from Clark [County]," Harrison wrote. "I am told that Mr. Badollett was present when McIntosh addressed them & advised them to vote for no one that had any confidence in me that I was their tyrant." Harrison added, "You will perceive the state to which Mr. B[adollet]'s mind had been worked up by party spirit when he suffered these gross impositions to be passed upon the ignorant French in his presence—I must own that it excited my utmost astonishment."[22]

The Harrison group ultimately came to believe Jennings had won through voting irregularities in Dearborn County. Although Jennings had a majority of votes according to the official returns, the Randolph forces argued that ninety-one votes should be subtracted from the total in the seventh district of Dearborn County because the returned copy of these votes was not certified by the poll keepers as the law directed. It was further contended that two districts in Dearborn County were prevented from voting at all. (Jennings claimed the precincts would not have made a difference in the election.)

Waller Taylor, a strong advocate for Randolph and a valuable ally of Harrison, noted the details of this circumstance in a letter to Randolph in 1809 shortly after the election: "There has no circumstance transpired to throw further light on the result of the Dearborn election since I saw you. Jennings's conduct is a little mysterious, but he still says he is elected. He states that he got 143 votes, that you got 67, and Jones an inconsiderable number; one township he had not heard from when he left there, but he apprehends no injury from that, as it was in part of the county the least populous. I expected the fellow would have been so much elated with his success that he would have been insolent and overbearing, but he says very little on the subject, and is silently preparing to go on to the city." Taylor further added, "Our meeting was not cordial on my part; I refused to speak to him until he threw himself in my way and made the first overtures, and then I would not shake hands with him. He has heard, I am told, of everything I said against him, which, by the by, was rather on the abusive order, but he revenges himself on me by saying that he never did anything to injure me, and professes esteem." Taylor thought Jennings "a pitiful coward, and certainly not of consequence enough to excite resentment nor any other sentiment than contempt. He may rest in peace for me. I will no longer continue to bother myself about him."[23]

Oddly, Randolph based his chief objection to the legality of the election on the grounds that Harrison's proclamation directing the election of a delegate was illegal. Randolph quickly made a legal protest and in the process placed the election in limbo. To Jennings's shock, a congressional committee would decide the election.

Harrison and his followers celebrated the 1809 Fourth of July in Vincennes by raising money to send Randolph to Washington, D.C., to personally make his case for invalidating the election. During the celebration, two toasts were made that clearly indicated the hatred harbored toward Jennings by this group. Harrison toasted, "Jonathan Jennings—the semblance of a delegate—his want of abilities the only safety of the people—three groans." Dennis Sullivan offered a similar type of cut, toasting, "Jonathan Jennings—may his want of talents be the sure means to defeat the anti-republican schemes of his party.'"[24] Badollet was apparently aware of this meeting and of the money raised to help Randolph, for he wrote Gallatin, "In the fumes of a fourth of July in the middle of a very mixed company, after some indecent toasts,

[Harrison] as some of his understrappers set a subscription going to defray the expenses of [Randolph] on the scandalous pretence that the subscribers could not consider themselves represented by the member elect."[25]

Despite this unexpected turn of events, a depressed but determined Jennings traveled to Washington, D.C., hoping for a chance to make his case in front of the congressional committee that now seemed to control his political fate. Thus, after the amazingly brutal 1809 campaign, another unforeseen hurdle emerged before Jennings could take his post as territorial representative. This bitter turnaround is touched upon in a letter from Jennings to Ann Mitchell: "My seat will be vacated in a few days, and in a few days after I shall be with you on my way to Indiana to again enter the lists of Candidates as we must try it over again as Paddy said when he got a drubbing. We are to have another election. The detail I will give you when I see you, till then must excuse. God knows I have hardly time to eat with everything hurrying. I am preparing a detailed account for the Pres of the Proceeding in my contested election."[26] Apparently, nothing was easy when it came to frontier Indiana politics.

At this juncture, arguments regarding the validity of the election grew incongruous in terms of previous political positions. Opponents of Harrison had argued earlier that the governor lacked the authority to call the election in the first place. Given the fact that Jennings did not want to go through another campaign, this contention now placed Jennings in the unusual situation of supporting Harrison's jurisdiction in this particular case. Conversely, Randolph found himself arguing against Harrison's authority. Jennings spoke of this strange circumstance in a letter to his friend Graham: "To support my election I had to advocate the Govenor's conduct and Randolph on the other hand was trying to prove it illegal by producing the laws of the Territory and of the United States. I made a long argument before the Committee of Elections to prove Harrison had acted legally—whilst Randolph produced laws enough to prove that his conduct was not legal, but still alledged, that the Govenor was not to blame because he could do no otherwise. This was playing off Camelion in earnest."[27]

The nation's capital can be oppressively hot and muggy in the summer. It was under such conditions that the issue of the fierce and bitter election for delegate to Congress from the Indiana Territory went before the national legislative body. In a letter to the chairman of the House Committee of Elections, William Findley, Jennings, as he had explained to Mitchell, found himself in the uncomfortable position of defending Harrison's action in holding the territorial election. Regarding the issue of voting abnormalities, Jennings argued the votes in question would not have changed the outcome. He further expressed confidence in the poll workers of Dearborn

111

County's seventh district, though acknowledging their failure to properly sign all forms. Jennings pointed to "irregularities" in pro-Randolph Knox County as well, placing votes there in question.[28]

Randolph, with his strong Virginia family connections, along with his support of the popular Harrison, walked confidently into the congressional committee room. He pled his case before the committee by mostly attacking Jennings's change of heart regarding Harrison's authority. "I am not a little astonished, sir, to see the change in sentiment which has taken place in that gentleman," Randolph said. "I did not expect a change of situation would have so metamorphosed him. He has chimed in with this faction in the clamor against this man [Harrison] in the vain hope of rendering him unpopular." Randolph then boasted to the committee, "Such a change should not be produced in me by personal considerations."[29] Much to Jennings's disappointment and Randolph's joy, the committee ruled the election was without authority of law and, consequently, Jennings was not entitled to his seat in Congress. The committee closed its report with the following resolution: "*Resolved*, That the election held for a delegate to Congress for the Indiana Territory, on the 22nd of May, 1809, being without authority of law, is void, and, consequently, the seat of Jonathan Jennings as a delegate for that Territory is hereby declared to be vacant."[30] Randolph believed the full House would likely concur with the committee's ruling, as was typical. Indeed, so confident was Randolph that a new election would be called that he rushed back to Indiana to start his campaign. A stunned Jennings stayed in the capital on the slim chance he might still persuade Congress to side with his argument. It turned out to be a wise decision.

The election committee presented its recommendation to the Committee of the Whole House in early January 1810. Extensive debate regarding the issue erupted over the next four days. During the early years of the American Republic, heated political debate often erupted over how flexible the Constitution was. Those who wished to expand governmental power called for a loose interpretation, while those who wished to restrict power called for a strict interpretation. Arguments focused almost exclusively on the right of Harrison to call an election based on a loose construction interpretation of the law. Interestingly, the election irregularities were considered irrelevant by the committee as well as by the House. The final vote of the entire House may have reflected many national leaders' growing concerns over the issue of slavery's expansion, or may have reflected, as Jennings believed, his power of persuasion. Whatever the reasons, the Committee of Elections's recommendation that Jennings's seat be vacated was defeated by the House by an 83 to 30 vote.

Jennings shared his personal views of the harrowing experience in a long letter to Mitchell: "My contested election has been to me a matter of considerable concern. Embarrassed in pecuniary matters, and pushed by my creditors, having little or no resort but to my own exertions, what could be my sensations under every apprehension that my seat would be vacated. The Committee of elections unanimously concurred in opinion that our Governor had no authority to order the election in which I was elected. This report of the committee of elections was concurred [with] when in Committee of the whole House." Jennings then explained how his adversary, Randolph, happily left to go start his campaign for a new election when the committee report came: "Upon this my competitor [Randolph], entertaining no doubt that it would pass in the same manner upon its final passage, left the City for the Territory to the end that he might take the advantage of me in electioneering." Jennings, however, doggedly pursued his goal of being recognized as the successful winner, telling Mitchell, "I had previously prepared the minds of some of the members both Republicans & Federalists to receive my attempts, and when the question was called for, I rose & in a lengthy argument opposed the final passage by remarking in my onset, that I thus did, because I conceived it a duty due from me to the citizens of the Territory." Jennings had touched upon a sensitive point—the right of the people to govern. The ensuing debate lasted three days and cost, according to Jennings, "not less than $2,000."[31]

The sudden reversal caused Jennings to observe, "Such a circumstance was never known before in the House & every member almost is expressing their surprize." The newly elected representative clearly saw the vote as a personal victory against Harrison. "Thus you see, Sir," Jennings bragged to his brother-in-law, "that I have exposed the conduct of my great enemy the Govenor, & have also been able to retain my seat in spite of all the sanguin expectations of my rivals & enemies." Of the hapless Randolph, Jennings noted, "My competitor under full impressions that my election would be set aside, will have made interest throughout the whole Territory before he learns his disappointment. Little indeed will he feel when he finds, that he has made interest for an election which will not take place for 16 months; when he thought & will declare will take place in the term of a few weeks."[32]

The fallout from this bitter competition lingered for some time. In a handbill issued by Randolph, the defeated Virginia native complained, "If at any time I have been led into indiscretion in my defense it has proceeded from the injustice and violence of my opponents."[33] In a circular addressed to the people, Jennings answered, "If Mr. Randolph succeeds in his wishes by fair means, without injuring me, reply upon it, that I shall never envy his success, nor take advantage of his absence to traduce him. But, if he expects to ascend the political ladder by slander and detraction, he ought not to be surprised if his borrowed popularity should forsake him and leave him, like other thorough-going politicians, without so much as the consolation of an approving heart."[34]

The anger generated by the election caused Randolph to challenge McNamee to a duel. The passive Quaker turned down the challenge, but Randolph still harassed the timid man by daily practicing "his shooting with pistols" around Vincennes.[35] McNamee evidently swore out a warrant regarding the threats, claiming "Thomas Randolph of the county of Knox hath challenged him to fight a duel, and that he hath good reason to believe and doth verily believe that the said Thomas Randolph will take his life and do him some bodily harm."[36]

Randolph was not so lucky when he challenged another anti-Harrison politician, the rugged William McIntosh. Badollet related to Gallatin how Randolph "attempted to cudgel in the streets a Mr. McIntosh . . . but to his great discomfiture he received two or three stabs from a dirk [dagger] to which McIntosh had recourse in his own defence." Badollet added in disgust, "Such is the State of Society here, such the manner in which the Governor watches over the peace and safety of the citizens!"[37] Randolph lay close to dying from the bout, but eventually recovered. In a letter from Dill to Randolph, the latter wrote he was happy to hear Randolph was "out of danger, and am really astonished you came off so well, considering the precipitate and inconsiderate manner you engaged." Dill hoped the incident would "have the effect of stopping the slanderous and libelous publications of that wretch, McIntosh, and if it does this you will not have risked your life for nothing."[38] But the political battle was far from over. As Randolph healed, he planned his next campaign against Jennings.

6

"Politicks are noisy deceptive subjects"

WITH MUCH EXCITEMENT, JONATHAN JENNINGS TRAVELED to the nation's capital in the early part of 1810 to finally take his contested seat in Congress. He found the capital hardly more than a wilderness village, with either dusty or muddy streets depending on the weather and with poor boarding opportunities. Regarding housing, one early secretary of the treasury observed, "I do not perceive how the members of Congress can possibly secure lodgings, unless they will consent to live like Scholars in a college or Monks in a monastery, crowded ten or twenty in one house, and utterly secluded from Society."[1] Further, Congress had not appropriated an adequate sum to improve or maintain the infrastructure, as Thomas Jefferson noted in one letter in 1807: "By the time the Pennsylvania avenue between the two houses is widened, newly graveled, planted, brick tunnels instead of wood, the roads round the squares put in order and that in the South front of the War office dug down to its proper level, there will be no more of the 3000 [dollars] left than will be wanting for more constant repairs."[2] In another report, Jefferson noted the sad shape of one wing of the Capitol building. "On opening the floors every part of the woodwork was found to be much more decayed than was ever apprehended; so that no one floor in the whole building could be considered as safe. Scarcely a single principal girder or beam was entirely sound, the tenants of the Oak joists were generally rotten,—and the only species of timber, which had at all withstood decay, was the pine and poplar of which the beams and the pillars were made."[3] Later, Jennings discovered that the boardinghouses where representatives stayed were often in states of decay as well.

Less than a decade before Jennings's arrival, the fledgling capital was described in negative terms by a number of visitors. Wrote one disturbed visitor, "If it is a city it is one in embryo, which will not come to perfection for these two centuries, if it ever does at all." "I am apprehensive," wrote another, "that as soon as he [President Washington] is defunct, the city . . . will also be the same." The summer heat was so bad, the writer went on to note, "that meat had to be slaughtered at midnight and sold before dawn. All liquors were kept in water. There were myriads of toads and frogs of enormous size, and other nauseous reptiles. The workmen lived in huts somewhat similar to booths, that I have seen erected at country races and fairs." Yet another outsider, who died a few months later of a fever, observed, "Very few persons who have been induced to visit this part stay here long, but disperse themselves over the other states."[4]

As Jennings always did when he found himself in a new setting, he soon grew lonely and despondent. To be sure, the twenty-five-year-old had gained many enemies as a result of the bitter 1809 election. In requesting support for another term as governor of the Indiana Territory, William Henry Harrison, for example, wrote the following comment about Jennings to a congressman: "I believe the poor animal who represents us in your house will also throw every obstacle in the way which his limited talents can create."[5] But most distressing for Jennings was the emotional pain he developed when not seeing or being around people he knew. To David Mitchell he wrote, "If I had not been very negligent myself I should be disposed to ask why I have not received a line from you since our last interview, but this is [a] matter of form, I only [hope] to draw a line from you if possible. . . . Give my tender love to my dear Sister," who Jennings added, "very frequently occupies my most tender reflections. The days we have spent together from the days of childhood to riper years, have been spent with as much real tenderness & affection as ever was realized by brother and sister." This constant harking back to his early and difficult childhood is typical of Jennings when he grew lonely. In this same letter he

labeled Mitchell his "Brother," and signed it as an "affec-
tionately and very sincere friend."[6]

When isolated, Jennings could be whiny, especially
when no one wrote him. In one correspondence, for
example, he grumbled to Mitchell, "What can be the reason I cannot hear from you. I have been expecting every
Mail or two to receive a line from you, but am as often disappointed. Surely Sister has no excuse, whatever may be
yours." Jennings grew so angry that he informed Mitchell
he was determined not to write him again until Mitchell at
least sent his name. Then he added, "When I sat down to
write this letter it was my full intention to have went
within one step of cursing a little, but I supposed you
might retort. But still you might scratch me a line or two,
confound it. I had very near written confound you—faith
I have wrote it—well then, confound you for a—why don't
you write me."[7]

To his friend, John Graham, he complained, "Why
have you not written me ere now?" A year later he was still
lamenting Graham's lack of correspondence, noting, "Since
my departure from Jeffersonville, I have not had the pleasure of one single line from you." In another letter he grew
sarcastic. "Since my arrival here I have heard nothing from
you. Are you dead, tell me so. If you are alive do for God
sake let me hear from you."[8] The lonely Jennings also continued to think about marriage. To Mitchell he wrote,
"Have you heard from Miss N[ancy] B[reading] since my

departure. I did intend to have written to her but you are so far off from my old walks that I suppose it would be inconvenient for you to transmit it and you alone would I entrust with such an embassy. If, however, you could so far conveniently oblige me I would yet do it."⁹

Jennings's loneliness eventually gave way to the hustle and bustle of national politics. The Washington, D.C., novice chose one focus in particular: getting rid of Harrison as territorial governor. A second problem that loomed concerned another difficult election campaign. Thomas Randolph had decided he would run again, and Jennings could bet that his old opponent would go to almost any lengths to even the political score. In order to work at both endeavors—getting rid of Harrison and winning the next election—Jennings attempted to establish a newspaper in Vincennes sympathetic to his cause. (The editor of the *Vincennes Western Sun*, Elihu Stout, had long been a Harrison supporter, although he usually printed all pieces sent to his paper.) Jennings wrote to Mitchell about the plan, asking his brother-in-law "to encourage Mr. Cooper to commence Editor at Vincennes. He will receive much encouragement at once, one man I am informed by letter will for the first year subscribe for 50 copies to any independent Pres. He will receive encouragement from both Indiana & Illinois Territory. By going there now he can at once take the lead and ever after keep it, when every year his establishment will become more valuable. I wish him to be there before the next meeting of the Territorial Legislature that he may obtain the Public printing."[10] Jennings failed in this particular effort. Whatever success in territorial politics Jennings might have, it would not come from the help of a friendly or even neutral newspaper.

Eliminating Harrison emerged as a difficult problem as well, but Jennings showed much optimism that his election victory had struck his adversary a particularly telling blow. To Graham he bragged, "Persevere my dear friend the day will shortly be ours—Our Govenor has depreciated at least 50 per cent since last spring and if he keeps pace for a few months in his sinking way, he will have to put into the sinking fund to prevent his value from being entirely lost." In another letter, Jennings, perhaps to show off his new status as an insider, then proceeded to give Graham some confidential information: "A quaker gentleman informed me that he had conversed with the Secretary of War, who told him that he doubted very much of the integrity of Harrison. . . . Depositions have been sent to [me] concerning the conduct of Harrison—I have laid them before the President and if he does not remove him I shall move against him in the House next month— Keep this to yourself for the present."[11] As it turned out, Jennings's optimism was greatly overblown.

In a lengthy letter to Secretary of State Albert Gallatin, Jennings set out another strategic attack on the governor, claiming Harrison had leased an important water source to cronies of poor character: "It would seem as if the Govenor has considered it as a matter of small importance indeed, seeing he has placed it in the hands of men, without any kind of security for the use they should make of it who, by the naked possession, without any kind of contract, claim to themselves the right of disposing of it at pleasure, at least for a term of years."[12]

Jennings found reassurance regarding his crusade against Harrison in the fact that Congress ordered a new territorial election in Indiana and that the new body that came out of this election quickly moved to repeal the indentured servant system Harrison and his followers had so painstakingly constructed. Other steps were also taken by the newly elected members to keep slavery and slaves out of Indiana. Harrison, accepting the new political reality, approved the measures. Meanwhile, Jennings busied himself serving his constituents.

Records show Jennings serving on a number of House committees. One report from a Jennings committee before that body came in the form of a bill that would have disqualified appointees of Harrison from serving in either the territorial house or the council of the territorial legislature. Jennings also served on a committee appointed to study the possibility of appropriating public lands, or proceeds from the sale of public lands, to open roads and canals "to the general interest of the union." Jennings specifically moved that the Committee on the Public Lands examine the possibility of creating one or more land districts from the cession lands recently negotiated by Indian treaties, allowing the selling of new land more quickly.[13] This was a wise move on Jennings's part, as settlers appreciated any political leader who made more new land available. The crafty Harrison, however, used the Indian treaty endeavor for his own political gain. In 1809 Harrison completed one of the largest land cessions in his tenure as Indian superintendent. The effort, however, did have a powerful downside.

Notwithstanding major opposition from some Miami tribal groups, Harrison was able to acquire nearly three million acres of choice land for the United States. In doing so, Harrison made more potential land available to the land-hungry settlers, but he created a situation of rising tension between Native Americans and white settlers. The latter problem would continue to make Harrison a valuable leader among the great majority of territorial settlers who feared the area's tribes. Some territorial residents, however, grew concerned about Harrison's actions toward the Native American population, seeing them as unnecessary and as part of a scheme to maintain his political hold on the territory.

John Badollet reported the results of the governor's work when he noted, "We are here in a singular and awfull situation, the warlike attitude of the Governor and the fears he has excited throughout this county—are such that a spark may produce an indian war."[14] In another instance of using the Indian fear factor as a political tool, Badollet observed how Harrison had used the ploy in trying to defeat Jennings in the 1809 election. "Even the idle rumor of an indian war," Badollet lamented, "has been made subservient to the same purpose [of defeating Jennings]." Indeed, as commander in chief, Harrison used his power to appoint officers in the "Indian crisis" to good effect. While, "the election business was going on," Badollet explained, "the member of the Assembly who had reported against slavery [General Washington Johnston] was made adjutant, although he knows as much about military affairs as I do about Pope's bulls. . . . The consequence was that he shifted side [for Randolph]."[15] But concerns about Harrison's political agenda were in the minority, as most citizens quickly rallied around the governor as a protector. Jennings later discovered that the territorial commander-in-chief position was one card Harrison possessed that Jennings could never quite trump.

Despite his ongoing fight against the ironfisted Harrison, Jennings did take time to help a friend. During the summer of 1810, Badollet became ill with a fever that lasted for several weeks. The hardworking, nervous land registrar reported his plight to his friend, Gallatin, and told of the timely help he received from Jennings (Congress was recessed at the time): "My distress was greatly increased by the circumstance of there being nobody here to whom I could or would delegate the business of my Office; at last, about the sixth or seventh week of my illness Mr. Jennings providentially arrived and by easing me of that trouble contributed to my recovery."[16] Badollet repaid his young friend by keeping him informed of political happenings in the region. That winter, for example, he wrote Jennings, telling him, "It is with a heartfelt pleasure my Dear Jennings that I am able to inform you that all the members of the Legislature from the Eastward [portion of the territory] started at the prorogation more your friends than ever and that R[andolph] notwithstanding his constant assiduities gained nothing & is by them thought less of than ever." Badollet went on to recite a detailed analysis of political happenings in the territory, including the fact that the governor, "as usual attended the house [of representatives] with a strict punctuality, taking share in the debates and suggesting arguments to members."[17]

By early 1811 Jennings faced what looked at first glance to be a tough re-election bid. Jennings wrote a political ally, Solomon Manwaring, telling him of his strategies for winning the contest. The plan called for Jennings to once again look to the eastern portion of the territory for enough votes to override the large majority Randolph would likely get in Knox and Harrison counties. "I have thought proper to ask of my friends in Franklin & Wayne

[Counties] the favour if they feel disposed, to have a meeting in each County, and resolve that they will support—
[Jennings] at the next election as Delegate to Congress,"
wrote Jennings. "I shall not mention the thing to any others but yourself and Mr. [John] Templeton and Capt.
[Thomas] McCoy and Capt. [Robert] Hanna. I do not
wish it to be known as being my request it would be made
a handle of by my enemies. But policy is necessary—Such
a measure will have the greatest weight in Knox County
because it is reported with great industry that Randolph
will get a majority with your upper Counties."[18]

Jennings also sought to weaken Harrison's reputation
with Manwaring by declaring, "The Governor is very
unpopular *here* [Washington, D.C.] and daily becomes
mor unpopular—I have received depositions and certifi-
cates with charges against Harrison and have shown them
to several members of Congress and they all tell I am
bound to give them their usual course and declare he
ought to be out of office—His political career is ended. I
shall lay the ground work of an impeachment before
ten days." Again, Jennings's confidence was overblown
regarding Harrison's weakness.Regarding his own political strengths, Jennings was more accurate. He confidently
asserted that "from what has been written to me from
every County in the Territory I think there is little doubt
of my next election. . . . I have written to several of
my friends to use every proper exertion, because if we

succeed, the Governor and his federal friends must go to the wall."[19]

Randolph was by no means unproductive during this time. Badollet detailed Randolph's intense efforts, noting the Harrison disciple "harangued the electors on the election ground and treated Jennings in a language too mean to be repeated outraging at once truth decency and our freedom of election." Randolph also attempted to attack Jennings by slandering Badollet and Nathaniel Ewing. To Gallatin, Badollet reported, "Mr. Randolph carried affidavits in every part of the Territory purporting that Ewing and I had written to you with a view to prevent the Memorial of our Legislature praying for an extension of credit to the purchasers of public lands." This lie, according to Badollet, cost Jennings, "a great number of votes."[20]

Randolph also used letters to the editor of the *Western Sun* as another tool against his opponent, describing Jennings's memory as "treacherous," his political skills as "adept in chicanery," and his arguments as "misrepresentations" of the truth. Randolph also contended that Jennings had not achieved one positive act for the betterment of the territory in his time in office, and accused him of lying about his work in committees.[21] Darker tricks were played as well by the Randolph forces. In Vincennes, Badollet reported "the Sheriff and the . . . clerk of the election had a third column opened [on the ballot] for *Jenni* as a third candidate, by which Jennings lost 46 votes, altho the French declared that they meant the man then in Congress [Jennings]." The dirty political trick, Badollet lamented, "has passed unchecked & the two men are applauded and high in favor for their ingenuity."[22]

One recent historian credits Jennings's re-election victory to his wise decision to ride the slavery issue again. "Jennings wasted no time," contends Brent Smith, "setting slavery in Indiana as the agenda for the election, an agenda that would send waves of resentment against Randolph for his beliefs about slavery." Randolph, for his part, quickly denounced the issue as a legitimate topic given that the legislature prohibited all slavery in Indiana in 1810. But Jennings "pushed the issue," Smith asserted, "realizing that the campaign could be won on that topic alone, regardless of how defunct it may be. His intuition proved correct; the voters considered slavery threatening enough to vote for Jennings, in spite of its prohibition."[23]

Perhaps just as significant was Jennings's ability to tap into the region's respect for anyone who seemed an advocate for the common man. As in their first bout, Jennings possessed much more strength in this area than the aristocratic Randolph. He had a gift for charming people and playing the political game. Isaac Naylor, a contemporary, noted, "I have said [Jennings] was no military man. This is true literally; but politically, he was a great captain. No military man ever enlisted his troops with more facility, organized them better, nor mustered them more skillfully than Jennings did his political friends."[24] Jennings himself was elated with his second victory over Randolph and the Harrison faction. He bragged to Mitchell that he was "elected by a majority of 2 to one almost." He happily added, "We go on well here and prosperity fills the sails of our Political Bark."[25] This contentment, however, would not last long, as Jennings returned to the kind of toil which so often left him feeling forlorn.

A letter penned in June 1811 indicated that Jennings still sought a mate. From Mitchell, he requested help to get a letter to an old love interest he had abandoned: "If Miss W. has reached the Western parts of Pennsylvania be particular in placing in her hand the enclosed letter. If she has not crosed the mountains, forward the letter by the first mail not forgetting to pay the postage for me . . . If Miss W. has, or should cros the mountains I shall expect you to advise me of it immediately."[26] We hear no more of the mysterious Miss W. after this particular correspondence, for the forlorn Jennings had found his helpmate.

Ann Hay was born in 1792 in Harrodsburg, Kentucky. The Hay family later moved to Clark County, Indiana. Jennings first met the seventeen-year-old Ann while campaigning in 1809, having come to her parents' home in Charlestown, Indiana, near where Jennings himself owned property. Jennings had gone there to enlist the support of John Hay in the 1809 contest. According to one account, Ann possessed "large brown eyes, reddish brown hair, a fair

skin and a graceful carriage. Her manners were most pleasing."[27] A rather romanticized version of their courtship contended, "Mr. Jennings, while exerting every effort for his
election, found time to keep in touch with Ann. On his
return from his first year in Congress he brought her a
miniature of himself, which Ann wore as a locket. It is from
this miniature that the portrait in the Indiana State House
was made."[28] The miniature mentioned is an important
artifact, as it shows a rather gaunt-looking man whose face
portrays a degree of worry. It is one of the few unromanti-
cized artifacts available regarding Jennings. (The official
portraits in Indianapolis that were based on this original
show an older and more confident Jennings.) The passage
is also interesting since a letter shows Jennings still pursu-
ing at least one other woman as late as two months before
his marriage to Ann in August 1811.[29]

Jennings was twenty-six and his new bride eighteen
years old. As noted, the marriage seemed rushed. One reason for the hurried wedding may be due to the fact that
Ann's father had recently died, leaving his daughter, to
some extent, at the mercy of the world. At any rate, the
marriage was an apparently quick decision for Jennings, as
evidenced in a letter he wrote to his sister seven days after
the wedding, happily telling her of the surprising circumstance. As usual, Jennings began the letter by chastising his
brother-in-law for not writing more often: "More than once
I have written to the Doctor, but he has as usual neglected

to let me hear from him." Then Jennings cut right to the exciting announcement:

> I have got news to tell you and expect that I have little to write you. What think you, is the news? It is important and such as you never knew before. Yes! I am married and have a wife, a little black eyed wife, and you another sister and a namesake, I wish you were acquainted with her. I am sure you would love her, not only for herself, but likewise for my sake. Her disposition is very similar to yours & what can I say more. In the course of another year I expect to take her with me to see you, and in the mean time I will bring you a lock of her hair, which will serve you as a memento of her who is near to the bosom of your Brother, and will of course, be near to yours. She is anxious to see you and have your friendship, and I am sure you have hers.[30]

Six months later, another letter written by Jennings to his sister indicated he had been giving much time to pondering the fairer sex. He related, for example, his notions regarding wives who have "scowling habits" by noting, "Some good wives say, for excuse, that they *mean no harm by it*, and *perhaps* they are candid in such declarations. Ha ha ha!!! For my part, I am determined, that my wife shall never act *such* a part, as to render it necessary, for her to excuse herself by saying 'that she means no harm by it.'" Perhaps aware that his record of success with the local girls back home was far from flawless, he ordered his sister "not shew this letter to any of the good matrons of your Town. I know that they generally in every part of the world, dislike criticism as much as the critics. But as they know nothing of my wife, they cannot act towards me according to their usual custom, by exclaiming with a pithy sentence, emphasized with a frown, *look at home*."[31]

Jennings had apparently taken his new bride to Washington, for he told his sister, "The City presents a very great variety of character this winter, yet notwithstanding the mirth & gaiety which the American Metropolis presents, I could spend my winters much more contentedly & happy with my little Ann at home. She is very well, and expresses frequently over her desire to be acquainted with you. As yet it is not my power to say when I shall return, but in the course of six or eight weeks I shall be able to inform you probably."[32]

There were two heavily romanticized versions of Ann Hay Jennings's brief sojourn in the nation's capital. Eleanor Long penned a children's book, titled *Wilderness to Washington: An 1811 Journey on Horseback*, that was purely speculation. Mabel Morrison, in her brief biography of Ann, tells of the couple's journey to the capital by noting, "Mr. Jennings, re-elected to Congress for the next two years, took his bride with him to Washington. The journey was made on horseback, the bride of course riding side saddle and wearing a long riding skirt. Her trousseau was in saddle bags. Tucked away in some secret hiding place, she had some pieces of money her mother had given her for Washington finery."[33] But Washington was not much of a city in 1811, as previously noted. A congressman's pay was six dollars a day, and items necessary for living were very expensive. There were also health concerns. The overprotective Jennings may have also feared that the bustle of the capital's environment would be harmful for his young and naive wife. Consequently, Ann did not stay long in Washington with her new husband.

In November of 1812 Jennings wrote his sister from the capital informing the Mitchell family that Ann would soon be arriving at their Pennsylvania home. Jennings wished his new wife kept from the local ladies, perhaps to save her from hearing stories of Jennings's failed courtships in that community. In the letter, Jennings came across as speaking of his wife the way a father might of a small daughter: "Shortly after this reaches you, I expect my little Ann will be with you. I wish and shall expect that you will exercise all that care and attention towards her which you as an elder Sister shall think proper. I do not wish her to visit any one connected with the connections of the Scott and Hogge family not even Mrs. Browne."[34]

Jennings seemed more than a little controlling of his "little" Ann. "She is entirely unsuspicious of the world and innocently artless and such I wish her to remain," he said. "The Society of the Doct and yourself will be the only part of your family at any time with which she will desire, or I wish her to be entertained." Jennings went on to lament how his political responsibilities kept him away from his husbandly duties. "I have often regretted that necessity compels me to be so much absent from her," he wrote. "It leaves her but too often an unprotected woman whose situation at all times is unpleasant. Be tender of her, she is tender and I need not tell you very dear to me." Jennings ended the letter with another warning to his sister to keep his wife away from bad influences: "Your Town I know is but too much disposed to ill natured remarks and censuring, and I wish my Ann to continue as she is, far out of the reach of their ill nature or that of any person to which she may be otherwise liable, being as she is, very little of a citizen of the world. . . . This letter is only for your own and if you choose the Doct's perusal; burn it."[35]

Two months later, Jennings, still in Washington, wrote his sister again: "Do my Sister afford every means reasonably within your power to make my little Ann happy as possible, till my return." Jennings's continued delight in his new bride was apparent. "I suspect you do not fully know her yet," he said. "She is generally reserved and very affectionate, and you will find quick in observation although she says very little of what passes. She is indeed a good girl, and if she does not render me happy, no other woman could." The letter also suggested Jennings had once more grown unhappy about being away from family and friends. Typically, his thoughts expressed a thinly veiled bitterness.

137

"You know I am not so very easily pleased," Jennings told his sister. "I have not received any thing from the Doct for a month nearly. He is very reserved this winter, but I can excuse him if he can excuse himself." Peevishly, Jennings also chastised his sister for requesting a New Year's present after not having written him in any consistent way: "I am now commencing a reprimand for you, because of your asking of me a new-years gift. Could you suppose you could get a new-years gift of me after having so long neglected to write me. . . . Oh you lazy Ann, you have not caught me, but I have caught you I suspect."[36]

Other personal matters affected Jennings during his second term as territorial representative. His friendship with Graham began to involve financial considerations and commitments. In one letter to Graham, Jennings declared, "I have for some time held myself, and do now hold myself, bound to advance you [160.00 dollars]."[37] Less than a month later, Jennings detailed his plan for having Graham come and aid him in farming activities in the Charlestown area:

> My wishes to get you to live with me is to oblige you and myself both. On that farm we shall have every convenience of life by industry. You will have no rent to pay, and everything that is raised shall contribute to your support and convenience with out costing you one cent. I shall furnish one man to work the whole year and you with bestowing your attention shall have the

one half of all the clear gain after deducting the
expences of necessary farming utensils. I will erect a
good saw-mill or a good Distillery, perhaps both, one of
them certainly within eighteen months, half the neat
[net] proceeds of which shall, after I erect them at my
own expense, for your care & oversight, be yours. To
the amount of what you owe me, I will then take at the
market price in corn or other grain when it is harvested
or whiskey so soon as it is distilled—Say no more about
it go and take possession the first of April if I be not at
home. You never had reason to complain of me I trust,
nor never shall. We will settle it to the satisfaction of
both, you need not doubt it.[38]

Three months later, Jennings loaned Graham eighty
more dollars and shared with him his confidence in being
reelected for a third term: "I am glad that the people stand
firm to the cause—Not that I am so anxious to be re-
elected, but for the sake more particularly of those who
have embarked with me—This however will be a secret
between you and I—Ewing writes me from Vincennes,
that I have gained much ground in Knox County and I
have not heard any contrary account from any quarter of
the Territory."[39] It is also to Graham that Jennings shared
the news of his wife's sickness, a condition that plagued
Ann until her death. "Mrs. Jennings has been unwell
nearly all the past Summer and fall," Jennings said,
adding, "I hope and intend to be with you soon after the
present Session shall terminate."[40]

Eventually, Jennings began to place more pressure on Graham to come live on a farm near or on the Jennings property. At this point Graham had apparently not made up his mind regarding the move. "I should be very glad to hear from you often and if you have not fixed a plan for your next summers, and after residence, prior to your settlement on your own domain, think of fixing yourself on my place for awhile," Jennings wrote. "It may be necessary however for you to come to a determination on this if you have not, before the Spring arrives, otherwise I may be induced to enter into arrangements which would not afterwards admit of the plan proposed to you." Jennings then proceeded to bring up the debt Graham owed him: "In making my arrangements for the ensuing summer, I have determined not to conclude finally, what they shall be, until I ask of you whether or not it will be convenient for you to pay me, any time next spring, any part, and how much of the sum which is between us." But Jennings immediately added, "If it will not be entirely convenient, or in other words, if it was not your expectation to be prepared for any reimbursement, before this letter reached you, I beg of you not to let my enquiry urge you the least, to any earlier payment."[41]

Graham promptly replied that he would not be able to repay the loan. But Jennings reassured his friend that he was "fully satisfied that you will return it as soon as you can and I hope, nay, you will not oblige me if you sacrifice any interest of yours to the object of repayment. I write as I feel. It was my friendship that induced me to loan, and that friendship undiminished, would be wounded if you were, because of my letter on this subject of a former date, to act as if I had required payment. Enough on this point." In the same letter, Jennings once more brought up the possibility of Graham living close to him. "If nothing else more advantageous presents itself to your view, my little property on Silver creek, will be always ready to yield to your comfort or advantage while you may be disposed to reside upon it," Jennings wrote. "If you have any ideas of that kind, communicate to me as soon as possible and you shall be accommodated."[42]

Ultimately, Jennings accepted the inevitable and wrote of his plan for helping his friend secure a federal job. "I have written to the Surveyor General at Chillicothe . . . with whom I am personally acquainted a pressing letter in your behalf, requesting to know, whether it will be in his power to employ you," said Jennings. "If not immediately, I have reason to believe, that ere long it will enable you to enter upon certain engagements which will enable you to command funds which will place you beyond the grasp of immediate necessity."[43]

It is a bit ironic, given Jennings's own complaints about Harrison's misuse of office, that Jennings understood and practiced the art of political patronage. To President James Monroe, for example, Jennings wrote a letter requesting a military academy appointment for one of Badollet's sons. Jennings described the youth as "about twelve or fourteen years of age, and his education confined to writing and reading the English language with a knowledge of arithmetic."[44] Occasionally, Badollet's nervous requests made him something of a pest; the rigid-thinking land registrar could go overboard with worry about things that likely would work out in time. In one example, the excitable Badollet reported to his friend Gallatin, "The last time that I saw Mr. Jennings I desired him to speak to you on, and obtain from you instructions respecting the manner of conducting the sales of land unpaid for, and making the proper entries in the book." Jennings told the worried Badollet "not to be uneasy," and that he would receive detailed instructions from Gallatin. "Yet I received nothing from you," Badollet complained to his friend. "Please to consider my situation, desirous of acting correctly and fearfull of doing wrong. I am in a situation very unpleasant."[45] For his part, Jennings always dealt patiently with his friend, perhaps out of respect for what Badollet had done for him during his early days at Vincennes. Jennings also recommended his brother-in-law, Andrew Hay, for the job of U.S. marshal for the Indiana Territory. Jennings labeled Hay "a man of education" who would "give general satisfaction" in the job.[46] In yet another letter to Monroe, Jennings offered one of his first political allies, James Bigger, for a military post.[47] In many ways Jennings was not much different than Harrison in his use of patronage. Such was the political reality on the Indiana frontier.

Jennings's most difficult political challenge during his entire time as territorial representative involved his ongoing fight with Harrison. The governor's hold on territorial politics seemed to have taken a mighty blow with Jennings's two victories over Randolph. Once in office, Jennings took every opportunity he could to attack the governor, calling for extended suffrage in the territory, for example, in his first term. Congress complied with his request in March 1811. Another sure sign of Harrison's fading power concerned the moving of the territorial capital from Vincennes to Corydon. Although the governor slowed the process with his veto powers, the move eventually took place in 1813. But despite Jennings's efforts, new factors emerged that once again brought Harrison to the political forefront.

Harrison's ongoing land deals continued to agitate Native Americans in the region. Two Shawnee, Tecumseh and his half brother, the Prophet, quickly became rallying points for many tribal groups in the territory. Harrison's substantial land negotiation successes stood at the core of this new movement's anger. Political opponents of Harrison, such as Badollet, Jennings, and William McIntosh, were also enraged by these treaty attempts, believing they stirred up the Native American population and were carried out for political advantage. Specifically, Badollet and his group believed Harrison's "alarms" made the general population more dependent on his military leadership. Conversely, the Harrison forces quickly seized the Indian threat as a tool for attacking the anti-Harrison forces. The Harrison faction, for example, accused Badollet and a few others of carrying out a *"treasonable* meeting, the object of which was to bring the indians" down on Vincennes. Badollet, in turn, complained how "Ewing & I are named as the chief conspirators." A trial of sorts was actually called for, made up of a "Harrison" jury. The governor's attempt demonstrated the level of hatred he had for his adversaries. "An indictment was first moved against us," Badollet reported. "Eight of the select band voted in the affirmative, but the other four ashamed of such proceedings opposed the measure, they tried next a simple presentment, which met the same fate and were at last disappointed in their last resource, namely that of carrying a vote of unqualified censure against the dangerous and treasonable interference of certain ill disposed persons in public affairs." Badollet marveled at "the unexpected return to honesty of four men from whom the Governor had a right to expect another conduct, rendered abortive his diabolical plan. But what will you think of a Country, where eight wretches can be found, capable of voting a bill of indictment, when no law had been violated, when in fact there was no statute to violate, in a word who could put respectable men, some officers of the U.S. upon their trial without either law or evidence?"[48]

In November 1811 Harrison led an army against Tecumseh and his followers. The Battle of Tippecanoe has been handed down in American history as a great and decisive victory. At the time, however, much controversy swirled around the event. Many territorial leaders died or were wounded in the battle. Jennings himself wrote his friend Graham lamenting, "Yesterday the Massacre on the Wabash was made known to me a horrid scene truly. Genl. Worthing[ton] in the Senate from Ohio has instituted an inquiry by raising a Committee in the Senate for that purpose. The inquiry is progressing."[49] Badollet described the carnage as "a bloody and dearly purchased victory." Badollet called Harrison's efforts, "an outrageous aggression on an unoffending & peaceable neighbor, and a wanton waste of treasure & blood."[50] Among those killed, according to Badollet, were "Joseph Daveiss, Wm. Mahon, Isaac White, and Thomas Randolph of the Light horse, Major Robb, Capt. Spier Spencer, Thomas Berry & Jacob Warrick of the Militia, and Capt. Bain of the Regulars, amounting in all to about 172 killed and wounded some mortally."[51] Badollet even confided to a friend that he believed the attack wrong and a horrible unjustice: "The little band of the Prophet and his brother, were not a banditti as I see them affectedly called in the public papers, they were a set of orderly sober and industrious men, who exhibited an appearance of decency and order worthy of imitation, whom we have driven to despair. . . . This act does reflect no honour on the boasted of justice of the United States." Perhaps with Harrison in mind, he added, "The powerful oppressing the weak is a spectacle which always distresses my heart."[52]

Lydia Bacon, whose husband served in the regular army at Tippecanoe, reported of the continuous deaths of many of the wounded: "A number of Soldiers have died of their wounds since their return, funerals [occur] often, sometimes two a day, very solemn is the sight & sound, for the coffins are followed by Soldiers, with their Arms reversed, marching to the tune of Roslin Castle beat upon

An artist's rendering of the fighting between American forces and Native Americans at the Battle of Tippecanoe on November 7, 1811.

146

Muffled drums."[53] Among the dead on the battlefield lay, as Badollet noted, Jennings's former political rival, Randolph. Waller Taylor, a close friend of Randolph and a political foe of Jennings, buried his friend by a large tree that he marked so that it might be found later by family members. General James Dill, Randolph's father-in-law, broke the sad news of the young man's death to his family: "It appears as if misfortune were to attend us in all situations and circumstances. News has at length arrived from the army. They have had a severe conflict, but a signal victory. . . . I wrote to you that Randolph had joined the army. I wish it had not been so, but it is now too late to wish. You will no doubt endeavor to support the trials heaven has thought proper to inflict. I wish I were with you, but that is impossible. . . . Many have been killed and more wounded, but there is one consolation for the friends of those slain— they died gloriously and in the arms of victory."[54]

Harrison's opponents tried to draw more political blood after the dubious battle by publicly praising the efforts of the regular army at Tippecanoe, while at the same time indirectly suggesting Harrison and the local militia were somewhat wanting in their performance. The public proclamation read in part, "Permit us to convey to you, and through you to the officers and men under your command, the exalted sense of the masterly and spirited conduct which you have displayed in the late engagement with the Indians at Tippecanoe." Conversely, the piece described the militia as "spirited but untutored" and undisciplined.[55]

Harrison supporters quickly attacked the pronouncement, declaring, "that the Militia which served under Governor Harrison were neither *untutored* or *undisciplined*, but in common with the Regular troops, they shared the attention of the Commander in Chief, and that by his *personal exertions*, both the Militia and Regulars were brought to a state of perfection in that kind of manoevering calculated for Indian warfare." The same broadside condemned a small band of anti-Harrison fanatics for threatening the success of the campaign by holding an earlier meeting questioning Harrison's tactics with the Prophet and his brother. (This was the meeting that caused charges of treason and disloyalty to be leveled against Badollet and a few others.) "We cannot but view as a most dangerous usurpation," the broadside said, "the meeting of a few individuals, not more than from seven to ten, in a private house, without any previous or public notice being given, and to pass resolutions . . . in the name of a neighborhood." The pro-Harrison declaration then condemned the group "*almost every one of whom are avowed enemies of the Commander in Chief.*"[56]

Harrison's devotees were quick on the attack against the governor's critics, especially Badollet and his immediate circle. The former came to lament to a friend about the growing tension, writing, "Dark hints are whispered about, we do not consider our lives as safe. I wish to God I was away. Never did I dream I ever would in America witness such things! We dread assassination, if ever those black calumnies come to be credited."[57] Badollet could count himself lucky. In 1811 a verbal attack was made on Harrison by McIntosh, who accused the governor of cheating the Indians out of their lands and, in the process, quickening their ill will. Harrison immediately brought suit for slander. Two judges abstained, likely because of their partiality for Harrison, leaving Judge Waller Taylor, a good friend of Harrison, in charge. The jury, also likely made up of pro-Harrison men, awarded Harrison damages of four thousand dollars.

Harrison did possess a sincere concern for his military people. He also understood the political advantage of helping the veterans of Tippecanoe, who made up the very fabric of the Indiana Territory. In a letter to Ohio senator Thomas Worthington, Harrison wrote, "Nothing in my opinion can be more just and politic than for the U States to provide handsomely for the families of those who were killed, as well as for those who were badly wounded."[58] The Battle of Tippecanoe eventually became a political reality for Jennings as well. He brought forth a resolution in the House in the early part of 1812 to pay one month's extra wage to all living veterans of Tippecanoe and to provide half pay for five years to families of those killed. Meanwhile, Harrison's actions at

Tippecanoe eventually won him great acclaim among the mostly upland southern population, who appreciated a man of action. Part of this support came from the fact that so many local men had served, and more than a few had died, at Tippecanoe.

The support of the common citizen for Harrison's actions grew with time. A well-respected Baptist minister and would-be poet, Isaac McCoy, for example, penned a poem entitled "An Eulogy on the Heroes of the 7th Nov. 1811," which appeared in the *Western Sun*. The piece strongly praised the sacrifices of those killed and Harrison's leadership. The first stanza declared, "Yes, let immortal honors crown/The heroes which to Shawnee Town/Did boldly march, and in the night/Did with the Indians bravely fight." Of Harrison, McCoy wrote, "May heaven protect our guardian friend/Wealth, health, and character defend/May he see many happy days/Whose deeds demands immortal praise." The last verse, one of fourteen, proclaimed, "O God, we bless thy mighty hand/Which still protects our guilty land/The spoiling of the serpent's nest/We hope will give our country rest."[59] A disgusted Badollet pronounced the piece a "nauseous effluvia of groveling stupidity."[60]

While Jennings attempted to use his position in the House to bring down Harrison, the governor's supporters kept him well informed about any activity against him. George Hunt, for example, wrote Harrison a lengthy letter in 1812, telling him facetiously, "We have had some Stir here about the remonstrance handed in to Congress by my friend Jonathan [Jennings] against Govr. Harrison. . . . I assure you Sir, I want to know the enemies of my country, for God knows we have had hard rubbing here." Hunt thought the pro-Harrison faction, "growing while I hope we may safely Compare the party of Honest Jonathan to the House of Saul" (that is, fallen). Hunt also reported Jennings was "very busy sending letters here" for the upcoming election. Hunt told Harrison, "from the Treatment you have received since the Battle we should not have been surprised if your Excellency had resigned," but then added, "for Gods Sake leave us not if you can possibly Bear with us, we know Jonathans drift."[61]

A twist of fate once again changed the political playing field. With the beginning of the War of 1812 with England, Harrison received an appointment as a major general in the U.S. Army. Jennings's joy over Harrison's leaving the position of governor is evidenced in a letter to Mitchell: "William H. Harrison is no longer to be Governor of Indiana. This I have from the most confidential and positive authority. This will be like a jubilee to many in the Territory, while others will care nothing about it and others, will be ready to bite their fingers for disappointment."[62] To his friend, Graham, Jennings wrote, "Harrison will no longer govern us Triumphed at last has virtuous perseverance."[63] Jennings could not keep from getting one more dig in at his old adversary. In mid-1813 he wrote Secretary of War John Armstrong complaining about Harrison's private use of military personnel in moving from the territory while Indiana suffered under Indian attacks:

> I have likewise received a letter from a gentleman of respectability and known to Mr. Griffin & Mr. Finley of the House, informing me that Genl. Harrison has ordered a Lieutenants command, from the western frontier of the Territory, of the Rangers, to convey some of his personal property from Vincennes to Cincinnati, which he had left at the first mentioned place since last August. How well such services may comport with the duty of a soldier I am not to decide, but when depradations are daily committed on that frontier by the savages, I cannot reconcile the alledged facts, to that protection intended to be afforded us by the general government, and to me they are irreconcileable to the high duties of a commanding general. I hope that my duty to the Territory which I am here to represent, will furnish a justification for my interference, while I must express my confidence, that the Secretary for the Department of War, will not suffer a transaction of the character I have described, to pass, by him unnoticed.[64]

Jennings himself apparently was not a hawk. He wrote his sister, Ann, for example, explaining, "War with England, my Sister, is not only probabl[e but], almost certain, and widows & Orphans, are among the minor evils attendant upon a state of war and consequent bloodshed. Many of those events, which have happened in almost every age, will soon transpire in our Country, unless our warlike disposition should commence and terminate." Jennings compared the conduct of those in favor of war to the domestic fights which "wives & old women too generally wage."[65]

Jennings's old nemesis, Waller Taylor, challenged him in his bid for a third term in 1812. Waller and the pro-Harrison faction began their attacks by first accusing Jennings's Pennsylvania-connected friends, Badollet and Ewing, of "highly criminal and improper" action regarding the service of the local militia at Tippecanoe. "The main object" of this scheme, asserted Badollet in a letter to Gallatin, was "to prevent Jennings' election & carry a certain Waller Taylor."[66] Once again, however, the election was fought out mostly on the pages of the *Western Sun*. A letter to the newspaper approved Taylor on "the basis of wide government experience, interest in serving the people, independence of thought, moral opposition to slavery, and a strong desire for Indiana statehood."[67]

Foes of Jennings attacked his record, charging, for example, that Jennings failed to acquire adequate compensation for veterans of Tippecanoe. Jennings defended his record by maintaining he had done all within his power to compensate the veterans and would gladly verify the information with anyone requesting the fact. Once more, Jennings's supporters brought forth the slavery issue. Specifically, backers of Jennings challenged Taylor about his opinions relative to slavery. Taylor quickly backpedaled, replying that he had never advocated the introduction of slavery into the Indiana Territory. The outcome was never much in doubt. By 1812 Jennings had established to a great extent his own political apparatus through his position in Washington and the power of appointment. Once more Jennings found himself a victor in the rough and rugged world of Indiana frontier politics.

In the spring of 1814, before his last campaign for a territorial seat in Congress, Jennings wrote his constituents, telling them of his frustration regarding accomplishing much in Congress. Like all good politicians, he blamed others rather than taking responsibility: "Since the commencement of the war, I have found it much more difficult to transact the business of the territory, than it was formerly. Besides the usual subjects of legislation, the pressure of public measures necessarily dependant upon a state of war, have had their effect. To preclude in a great measure the ordinary opportunity of war we must calculate on privations, and like others we should learn to bear them." Jennings then touted the work he achieved on behalf of the people of the territory despite obstacles. "The defence of the frontier of our territory has not been neglected," Jennings claimed. "With much satisfaction, I have learned that the rangers as far as could have been reasonably expected, have guarded the frontier inhabitants from the merciless attacks of the savages. They will be continued in service as long as their services will be necessary and for this purpose a law has passed during the present session."[68]

Jennings also wisely announced that a "law has passed giving a further time to those purchasers of public lands." Land-hungry settlers would be glad of this. Jennings also told of his political intentions: "I had intended to decline being a candidate at the ensuing congressional election. I even went so far as to tell some of my friends, confidentially, that I wished to decline, and no doubt some have calculated on it. It was my intention, and I certainly should have declined, if most substantial friends in different parts of the territory had not urged me again to become a candidate. Since I have been honored with your confidence and the discharge of a trust so important, my first object has invariable been, to render you every service in my power." Jennings ended his report with an indirect shot at his old foe, Harrison. "So far as my present views are connected with public life, they have for their object the welfare of our territory more particularly; and the promotion of virtuous men," Jennings said. "Fellow citizens, it is worthy of our attention and it should be our study, to dispence with every prejudice possibley and unite in forming for ourselves a character on liberal and virtuous principles which will insure our future happiness and prosperity."[69]

The election was a walkover. Jennings won an easy victory over Elijah Sparks of Dearborn County, who had
been serving as attorney for the United States in the territory during the past year. Apparently there were no particular issues involved: Sparks presented only that his goal
was "to assist in raising up and establishing the equal rights
of man—of all men, above the iron grasp of tyranny, the
yoke of despotism, and the drudgery of oppression," while
Jennings pointed to his record of service during his four
and a half years as delegate.[70] Again, the political machine
Jennings had developed proved invincible.

The twenty-eight-year-old Jennings had grown somewhat cynical about politics, telling Mitchell, "I would try to
conceal every feeling, no matter how unpleas[an]t. It is
the first Principle of political philosophy."[71] Jennings also
seemed to grow more and more depressed in the nation's
capital. Of the city itself, he noted to Jesse Lynch Holman,
"Once more I have reached the metropolis of our country
where gaiety, formality and the rounds of fashionable folly
are the order of the day with the people of high life. Here
the cheerful simplicity of rural manners are unknown as
well as the pleasures they afford to the circles of domestic
life." Jennings went on to complain that "these swarms of
fashionable empherons, neither think nor speak, without
consulting whether or not it be the *mode*. Here every face
wears a smile either feigned or real, though poverty
unveiled, retrenches the necessities of life to give means

to make a *figure*. How disgusting? With my little stock of skill in human [nature], I have never thought myself safe to attempt forming one friend, more than, what we may call, civil folks."[72]

To Mitchell, Jennings complained, "Your letter of the 22nd I have received. It is the first for a *long time* but I hope it will not be the *last* for a *long time*." On the up side, Jennings told him about his happy marriage. "I am happily married and can rejoice in reality that my judgment was able to controul natural disposition in the important measure of matrimony. I might have married *a name*, a *fortune*, but I have married a woman, a *very woman*. A woman of great goodness of disposition, of *common sense* and prudent. Lovely enough for me. I shall be happy soon to enjoy the balance of my time in a retirement where neither poverty or riches, good or bad fame shall be able to disturb, improperly, my retreat." Then, in a sudden bit of reflection, Jennings added, "To be happy in this world is far beyond my expectations, so much so that I scarcely wish it. To be contented is my greatest ambition."[73] This somber outlook was shaped by the death of his only surviving parent, sickness within his family, and other ongoing problems.[74]

It was toward the end of his first Washington service that signs of Jennings's drinking problem emerged. To his sister, who was traveling from Pennsylvania to the East Coast, he advised, "I have nothing to relate that could interest you, only to urge you to lay up a sufficient stock of *spirits*, to bear you again over the mountain." Then he calculated, "More will be required, and more you must have to stand the heat and fatigue which we shall have to undergo."[75] It was apparent that in Jennings's mind, alcohol solved a number of physical problems.

In a more telling letter to Mitchell, he related his thoughts on his loneliness, on an illness common to those who drink too much, and on the spirit-crushing effects of politics: "Your letter of the first inst: I have received and with you I agree that it is a long time since I have heard from you ere this. The miseries of my friends I like to know and feel although the effects are entirely negative so far as happiness or enjoyment is to be derived from that source. I never will suffer myself to believe that you measure me by your letter either in length or numbers. I have myself hardly time to write a line to a friend and I have been a very ill with the Jaundice of which I am but partially recovered." (Adult jaundice is often brought on by alcoholism.) Of the political life, Jennings mused, "Politicks are noisy deceptive subjects, yet every man for himself at least ought to consider himself the guardian of his political safety, having a common share in the great fund of national prosperity or its reverse. We are in a shameful wretched state. What more could I say, more I ought not to say."[76]

Jennings's correspondence suggested that he possessed a fundamental aversion for routine. At the same time, new circumstances almost always brought on depression. Nor did his surprising successes bring him any peace. In early 1816 he penned a letter to a political ally: "You have no doubt a heavy charge . . . to taste the *fruits* of *much* absence from your home and family, from your beloved retirement, from your groves and gardens and dreams of rural felicity."[77] Although he spoke of his friend's pain at being away from the things he loved because of political responsibilities, Jennings was surely thinking of his own unhappy situation.

By 1816 Jennings had served three full terms as Indiana's territorial representative. The young upstart had yet to taste political defeat, and he had outlasted his bitter opponent Harrison. In the political vacuum left by Harrison's departure, Jennings stood alone in the field as the most high-profile political leader in the territory. Now a new challenge loomed for Jennings, one that was destined to make his name forever a part of Indiana history and bring him some relief from the boredom that so often troubled him.

7

"I hold an office . . . capable of yielding but little satisfaction"

AT THE CORE OF THE POLITICAL HEART OF HOOSIER FRON-
tier people beat the desire for complete self government.
As Indiana historians John Barnhart and Donald Carmony
noted, the actualization of total self-government "could be
fully achieved only by statehood."[1] The end of the War of
1812 and the peace that followed brought more settlers
into the territory and moved Indiana closer to the prize of
statehood. Many, such as John Badollet, had called for the
status several years before it finally came in 1816. Badollet
and other statehood supporters perceived statehood as a
way of overcoming the territorial despotism of Governor
William Henry Harrison and his faction. Badollet, for
example, explained in a letter how "a member of the
Legislature, after having in conversation with me, des-
canted with much heat on the evils of Territorial
Government, and in particular on those we Suffer, concluded by observing that our only means of salvation was

to enter into a state Government." The concerned citizen then asked Badollet "to draw a memorial to Congress and desired me in writing it to dip my pen *in gall.*" Badollet soon "went to work, not with gall, but what I thought a decent degree of vigor, telling boldly some wholesome truths."[2] This first attempt, however, failed. Harrison and his forces still held too much sway at this time.

Even by 1816, Thomas Posey, appointed to take Harrison's place as territorial governor in 1812, strongly opposed the move to statehood. In a letter to the U.S. secretary of state, Posey, a sixty-four-year-old Virginian, suggested that the people of Indiana would not be ready for self-government for at least three years; that is, not until another term of office for Posey was up. His concerns involved the lack of resources and distinguished leaders: "Some of our Citizens are very restless to go into a State government. I wish the people were well prepared for the measure, but I may say with propriety that at least two thirds, or three fourths, are not able to contribute but very little, if any thing to the Support of a State; and there is also a very great scarcity of talents, or men of such information as are necessary to fill the respective Stations, & offices of government." Reasoned Posey, "three years would be short enough to place the Territory in a situation for the change. But so anxious are many, that no doubt they will be ready to accept of any terms. We have numbers sufficient, & that is all we can boast of."[3]

IHS, P130

Thomas Posey.

In reality, Posey likely carried the same political agenda as his predecessor. He came from the same background and possessed similar tastes to that of the aristocratic Harrison. "It was only natural," asserted Jacob P.

Dunn Jr., "that the personal friends of General Harrison became Posey's personal friends; and in equally natural sequence he fell heir to Harrison's political estate as well as to his office."[4] Doubtless, Posey strived to perpetuate the Harrison political machine, as would have all the officeholders and cronies from the former regime. But the attitude displayed by Posey, and the remnants of the Harrison apparatus, was no match for the wave of new immigrants who touted the banner of Jeffersonian democracy and the common man—a banner Jennings clearly carried in Indiana. Politically, Jennings was well situated to take advantage of the political situation. By 1815 the territory had a population of more than sixty thousand, a major requirement for statehood. In December 1815 Jennings presented a petition to Congress "praying" for Indiana statehood.

After Harrison's departure, his faction could only gain ground by attacking Jennings and the statehood initiative, whether directly or indirectly. For example, Elihu Stout, the publisher of the *Vincennes Western Sun*, brought forth an editorial in April 1816 defending the honesty and service of Harrison by declaring the governor would be remembered long after "his puny and contemptible slanderers will be thought of only to be scorned." Stout also condemned Jennings's ongoing congressional inquests into Harrison's expenditures as pointless.[5] Anti-Jennings writers sending opinions to the *Western Sun* further disputed the advantages of statehood, arguing that the expenses of a state government would not justify the benefits. One writer estimated statehood would cost the taxpayers of Indiana $30,000 per year. The concerned citizen ended his argument with a harsh warning: "I am told this same Jonathan Jennings will at our ensuing elections be a candidate for the highest office, governor . . . shall we not, fellow citizens, very correctly eliminate him by suffering his retirement to the plough?"[6] But the pro-Harrison *Western Sun* was now out of step with the rest of the territory. Its vast supply of ink could no longer guarantee the old political regime's success.

In early 1816 Jennings reassured eager constituents that the petition for statehood had "met a very favorable reception." Confidently, Jennings told a political associate, "In relation to Indiana, and its probable change of its form of government, I have no doubt a law will pass at some period of the present Session of Congress, for the purpose, on terms as favourable, if not much more so, than have been acceaded to any other Territories of the U. States."[7] His own aspirations for the governor's position, he claimed to his friend, were less certain. Political opponents knew better, however. One wrote to the *Western Sun* accusing Jennings of neglecting his duties as congressman while he worked for statehood.[8] Other anti-Jennings writers soon joined in, but Jennings's popularity, now tied to the statehood movement, could not be stymied. Congress passed the Enabling Act for statehood on April 15, 1816. Jennings announced the passage two days later in an open letter to the *Western Sun*, telling the public, "The act to enable the people of Indiana to form a constitution and state government has passed both Houses of congress, and will undoubtedly receive the President's signature."[9] Statehood lacked only a constitutional convention to create a government under which Hoosiers would live. At this convention in Corydon, delegates very quickly elected Jennings as president. With this position came the power to appoint committee chairs. More importantly for Jennings, the majority of delegates elected to frame the new state constitution were members of the Jennings faction (that is, anti-Harrison).

Two aspects of Indiana's first constitutional convention have long caught the eye of historians—the disputable lack of political factions and the "southernness" of the convention members. Earlier historians, such as Jacob P. Dunn Jr. and Logan Esarey, typically offer an idealized view of the convention. Later historians, such as John Barnhart, Donald Carmony, and Andrew R. L. Cayton, provide more critical assessments. Esarey claimed he could not discern the existence of political parties working during the sultry summer of 1816 when forty-three delegates came to hammer out Indiana's first state government. Esarey pointed out, for example, "In the selection of delegates to the convention no definite political parties

166

nor political issues appeared . . . . Even the old issues of slavery and aristocracy belonged to the era of territorial strife. The slavery question seems to have played a very minor part in the selection of delegates and in the work of the convention."[10] Conversely, Dunn emphasized the lingering ghost of the slavery issue, which he believed still hovered over Corydon, and the heroic work of Jennings and his supporters in defeating this evil. Barnhart and Carmony thought Esarey was entirely wrong and Dunn missed "the larger issue of a democratic state and a democratic society." The latter two historians are also more realistically blunt in their assessment of what drove Jennings and his supporters: "The popular party, which was the driving force in the statehood movement,

The capitol building at Corydon.

included persons who had been appointed to few if any offices [by Harrison] and who, no doubt, wanted to have such honors."[11]

Ironically, many there did not disagree with Posey's earlier assessment regarding the want of intellect among delegate members. Indeed, much has been said about the lack of distinction among the delegates. Barnhart and Carmony believed the Harrison group possessed what few articulate men could be found there at Corydon. Conversely, they believed the Jennings faction "was representative of the frontier farmers, was chosen from the people, and did not contain so many prominent leaders."[12] One convention member, James Dill, a Virginia aristocrat and Harrison supporter, noted, "Talents are most damnably scarce here—and he who has but a moderate share is looked upon as a great man."[13] Even John Badollet, a Jennings ally and his former mentor, judged the group to be greatly wanting. "It is unfortunate," Badollet wrote a few years after the event, "that, when called upon to form a constitution a territory is in the most unpropitious circumstances to success for the want of men of intellect and political knowledge . . . . This was woefully verified in our case, for though our convention contained several thinking men, the majority was composed of empty bablers, democratic to madness, having incessantly the *people* in their mouths and their dear selves in their eyes."[14]

While the negative assessment regarding ability at the convention held a majority, this was not the only view. According to Jennings, one delegate, William Hendricks, thought "no country ever presented more [worthy] candidates for its population, than does Indiana, to lay the foundation of our proposed state Fabrick."[15] In that same vein, historian John B. Dillon believed the delegates "clear-minded, unpretending heir of common-sense whose patriotism was unquestionable and whose moral was fair."[16] While Dunn envisioned Jennings "a young Hercules, stripped for the fray, and wielding the mighty bludgeon of 'No Slavery in Indiana,'" his leadership, assessed two other more recent historians, was "not evident in the convention."[17] A more recent critical evaluation of Jennings could also serve as a possible description of others there at the convention who believed as he did. Jennings, noted Cayton, "believed, in a vague but intense and impetuous fashion, in the rights of white men, the value of popular democracy, and the evils of slavery . . . . Like his allies and supporters, Jennings held no brief for pure democracy. Rather, he believed that society should function so as to allow naturally talented men to stand out among their brothers."[18]

Another aspect often mentioned by historians concerns the "southernness" of the delegates. "The nativity of the members of the convention illustrates the extent to which Indiana Territory was connected with the South,"

argued Barnhart and Carmony. "The place of previous residence of these representatives not only emphasizes this
point, but reveals that their origins were in the Upland
South or in the southern part of what Frederick Jackson
Turner called the 'Old West.' In other words, they
belonged not to the planter class but to the democratic
farmer people."[19] Much has been made of this upland
South connection and the rejection of slavery. Such an
interpretation may be somewhat amiss, however, if it
ignores where delegates came from before they settled
in Indiana. Badollet, originally from Switzerland, and
Jennings, born in New Jersey, had created an alliance
of sorts in Pennsylvania, along with Nathaniel Ewing,
before going west. Jennings likely knew John K. Graham
and William Hendricks in the Keystone State as well.
Pennsylvania, while not necessarily the state of birth for
these men, still provided the environment that shaped
their political and cultural understanding. The more
diverse and somewhat more sophisticated culture found in
Pennsylvania no doubt greatly influenced these men.

As convention president, the thirty-two-year-old
Jennings gazed over the Corydon gathering with a great
sense of satisfaction and triumph. He had certainly jour-
neyed a long way from Vincennes. A few of those sitting
before him, such as Dill, were old enemies from earlier
political campaigns. Now they were forced to watch as
Jennings presided. Hendricks, a six-foot-tall Pennsylvanian

with red hair and blue eyes, was elected secretary of the convention. Hendricks, a representative from Clark County at the convention, had attended the same college in Pennsylvania as Jennings and his brothers, and like the Jennings family, had been raised Presbyterian. Badollet was one of the representatives from Knox County and served as chairman of the committee to prepare a preamble and bill of rights. Pennsylvania native John Johnson, whose run for territorial representative had split the votes and gave Jennings a victory over Thomas Randolph in 1809, served as chairman of the committee on the distribution of governmental powers. Jennings's close friend Graham was made chairman of the executive department. All committee leaders had been approved by Jennings.[20]

The delegates certainly did not reinvent the wheel. Following the instructions of the Northwest Ordinance and the blueprint of other state constitutions, the group finished their work in nineteen days. More than 90 percent of the wording of the final draft came from other constitutions. Badollet's preamble, for example, was almost entirely that of Ohio's state constitution. The group also acted out of a need to rise above typical political infighting while carrying out the business of the convention. Rules of decorum, for example, included the directions that when the president spoke, "none shall walk across the room; nor when a member is speaking enter on private discourse, or pass between him and his chair." Another rule forbade the delegates from indulging in "personal reflections" or name-calling in passing portions of the constitution as they came under deliberation.[21]

Given that the majority of delegates were Jennings's followers, the only difficult issue looming over the group involved the future status of African Americans. Slavery had already been denied by territorial legislation and was quickly reinforced by the new constitution. A troubling question remained, however, regarding the situation of indentured servitude. Initially, a move was made to prohibit indentured servitude of adults and illegal indentures "of Negroes or mulattoes whither made within or without the state except apprenticeships." In the Committee of the Whole, however, the law was reduced to a simple declaration that "any indenture of any negro or mulatto hereafter made, and executed out of the bounds of this state [shall not] be of any validity within the state."[22] This change, a cruel compromise, preserved the indenture contracts already in existence and reflected the fact that the old Harrison faction still carried some punch. Thus, the political reality was much different than suggested by earlier historians such as Dunn. Slaves would be present in Indiana almost to mid-century. Records show, for example, thirty-two slaves in Vincennes in 1830. Furthermore, black Hoosiers found themselves unwanted in the state and, for many years, faced several laws that greatly restricted their rights.[23]

Other laws passed at the Corydon convention excluded Negroes, mulattoes, and Indians from the militia. Another article restricted the all-important right of voting to white adult male citizens of the United States. Clearly, the conduct of the delegates demonstrated not only hostility to slavery but also a desire to limit the migration of black Americans into the state. Hoosier whites had long struggled with the question of black residency, as evidenced by a petition written from Harrison County to Governor Posey in 1814 asking in part for the governor "to use your influence to have removed from this neighborhood a hoard of free Negroes that has lately made a settlement among us. You Sir, may form an idea of the disagreeable situation we will be in when we have nearly one hundred of those wretches in our bosom. . . . Believe me my dear Sir, my Paradise will be converted into a Hell, if those Negroes remain in this neighborhood and at this critical period a frown from you will answer the purpose."[24] The lack of change on behalf of Indiana blacks at the convention in 1816 demonstrated that many delegates still carried the same prejudice of those who signed the 1814 petition.

In early July 1816 a special announcement appeared in the *Western Sun*: "We have also understood that Thomas Posey and Jonathan Jennings are candidates for the office of governor." With the campaign officially under way, the letters again began pouring into the newspaper.

173

Some brought up old charges. In an open letter to Jennings, "A Citizen of Gibson County" asked several biting questions respecting his behavior while in Washington, D.C.[25] The bias of the paper was evident. Letters appeared endorsing Posey because of his experience as territorial governor, but none appeared supporting Jennings. Jennings, however, had reached the pinnacle of his career. Indeed, the *Western Sun* declared Jennings governor by "a handsome majority" before the votes were all in.[26] Jennings and his wife prepared to move to the new state capital at Corydon.

Living in Corydon became both a blessing and a curse for the couple. Ann Hay Jennings's family lived nearby, and the Mitchells finally moved to Corydon in 1818. The small community had little of the hustle and bustle of Washington, D.C., which Jonathan Jennings had so despised. One state representative described the village as containing buildings "not exceeding one hundred in number" that "were either cabins or of hewn logs." But the size of the village and its remoteness greatly limited a number of important services. "As the town was but little visited except during the sessions of the legislature, there was then often a large crowd, while the means of accommodation were not in proportion," the representative noted. "The supplies came from Louisville, twenty-five miles distant; but the state of the roads and streams was such that no regularity could be relied on."[27]

Posey also had complained of the capital's remoteness, writing to the territorial legislature, "I wish you to communicate to your honorable body that the delicate state of my health will not admit of my longer continuance at this place [Corydon]. I find myself badly situated on account of the want of medical aid. My physician is at Louisville, and I have taken all the medicine brought with me. The weather is moderate now, which will be favorable to my going to Jeffersonville, where any communication that the two houses of the Legislature may have to make will find me."[28]

As Posey's letter suggests, sickness often prevailed in Corydon, and Ann seemed especially vulnerable. In Jennings's second year as governor, he reported to Indiana Secretary of State Robert New, "I am detained here, contrary to my expectations, by the sickness of Mrs. Jennings, and have therefore to solicit you to forward to me at this place, in the mode you did lately, all commissions for the West, which are or should be executed on your part."[29] To the Mitchells, Jennings bemoaned, "Ann has enjoyed very imperfect health and also suffered considerable pain. She is at present tolerable."[30] Another letter, written by Ann's brother, Andrew Hay, in late 1820, reports "Mrs. Jennings is not well."[31] Ann's health deteriorated during her husband's tenure as governor.

Jennings himself hinted at his own unhappiness while residing in Corydon and serving as governor, writing

175

David Mitchell, "My situation is not very pleasant. I am too young for the situation I occupy. It excites too much jealousy." As usual, when sad, Jennings drifted into depression: "Rugged and difficult are the p[aths] through which our phantoms lead us in the mazes of life and its turmoil and disappointments . . . . How mysterious are the events of time under the guidance of an all wise beneficent providence. The great empheron of creation, man, expects much and realizes little in this life but anxiety, pain and fatigue." Typically, Jennings also asked his brother-in-law and sister to come live near him: "Tell Sister Ann, that unless you remove to this country I never more shall expect to see her. An unpleasant thought. She was the constant companion of my childhood for many years, and to me, is, very, very dear."[32]

A drawing of Jonathan Jennings's home in Corydon.

By 1817 the Mitchells were seriously considering the idea of coming to Indiana. In March 1817 Jennings reported to David, "I received a few days ago your letter making enquiry with regard to the prospect of Bookselling in this State and the Territory of Illinois. It cannot be good in Illinois, and I am disposed to think it would not be a *good* business in this State, though probably some would sell at Vincennes and the surrounding country. In Vincennes however there are several physicians, some only, as I understand, of them, are regularly bred."[33] The Mitchells moved to Indiana in 1818.

Mabel Morrison, in a short biography of Ann Hay Jennings, offers a rather romantic version of the couple's state capital years: "Governor and Mrs. Jennings did much entertaining, and the little sister's grand-children heard many stories of the visitors, who, often accompanied by their colored servants, came to the 'Mansion' usually on horseback, but sometimes in stages. Their grandmother told of the many candles lighted, the big dinners served. The guests, legislators, judges and travellers talked on many interesting subjects at the table, and around the fireplaces, for it was a day of much discussion." Perhaps the most important guests entertained by the Jennings were President James Monroe and General Andrew Jackson. Morrison relates, "When word reached Corydon of President Monroe's approach, the citizens went out en masse to meet him. He arrived at 11 a.m., June 29, 1819, and left the next morning at 5 o'clock. Governor Jennings, General Tipton and others accompanied him to the ferry that carried him back to Louisville." The *Indiana Gazette* also carried the story on the Monroe visit: "Mr. and Mrs. Jennings gave a dinner at 4 o'clock to honor their guests. A roast pig with an apple in his mouth graced the table. Venison was another meat served. Cherry pie was a dessert. Mrs. Jennings' brother Andrew and wife and young sister Julia were among the guests."[34]

Jennings served as governor during a time when the importance of political parties had briefly faded, especially in the Old Northwest. At the height of Jennings's career, around 1816, almost every Hoosier politician was aligned with Republicanism. As Adam Leonard related in his definitive essay on personal politics in Indiana, "In this period all claimed to be Republicans; none would accept the name Federalists. The elections were waged about the personality of men or upon local or passing issues."[35] Barnhart and Carmony concurred, noting, "No avowed Federalist ever held any office under either the territory or state."[36]

The 1822 congressional election in the state's first district underscores the damage that occurred if a candidate successfully hung the label of Federalist upon his opponent. In this contest, Charles Dewey, a later benefactor of Jennings, stood accused in a district newspaper of being "a violent Federalist" who had taken part in the highly unpopular Hartford Convention in 1814. The meeting represented an attempt by some New England groups to pull that region out of the union in response to the South's and West's determination to fight a war with England, the War of 1812 being very destructive to New England's economy.[37] Dewey frantically attempted to refute the charge, writing to the same paper, "The insinuations that I was a member of the Hartford Convention, or had any connection whatever with that body, are false. I call upon my accuser for proof. I solicit the people not to suffer me to become the victim of accusation unsupported by evidence, or even a name."[38] Despite an eventual number of letters to the newspaper proving the charges to be false, Dewey lost the election by a wide margin.

Tagging an opponent as a violent Federalist, however, rarely happened in Indiana. In the absence of national party issues around which a candidate could rally supporters, personal politics came to dominate the voting scene. Indeed, the duel forces of frontier democratic spirit and personal popularity, the latter the primary element of personal politics, often increased the intensity of Hoosier elections. One Hoosier diarist commented on the fervor created by one local/state contest when he observed, "the people much agitated about the approaching Election. There is much canvassing the character of candidates and their Eligibility. There is hardly a man in town but that

179

offers for some office."[39] Letters of the day also convey the turmoil created by elections. "Politicks is Raging here," wrote one alarmed Hoosier.[40] Another penned, "our election . . . was warm—nay! it was bitter."[41]

Political handbills, or broadsides as they were called, flooded Hoosier communities prior to election time. In the same vein as newspapers, broadsides more often than not brutally attacked the character of a candidate. John Ewing, for example, explaining why he had produced such a document, wrote, "HENRY DUBOIS has left me no alternation other than to shoot him, as I might a dog, or to adopt this mode to expose his baseness."[42] Indiana citizens seemed keenly aware of their unusual penchant for politics. Calvin Fletcher, who came to Indiana from the more reserved region of Vermont, complained politics were "a subject . . . of every newspaper and the chit chat of the counting room of the merchant the bar room of the inn the fire side of the farmer and the work-shop of the mechanic."[43]

Not every Hoosier, however, got into the election spirit. One who signed his name "Farmer" in a letter to the editor of the *Evansville Gazette* complained, "Scarcely a day passes over my head but a portion of it is spent with some person who is out electioneering. I shall never cease to complain while I am so constantly teased, vexed, and harassed as I am now on the subject of elections and with candidates."[44] Nor did the election process insure that the ablest candidates would necessarily be chosen. "I am extremely mortified to inform you," Benjamin Noble wrote John Tipton, "that Franklin County has elected two representatives, neither of whom can write a sentence of English, over a man who has . . . faithfully, honestly & assiduously served his constituents."[45]

Prior to any Indiana election, newspapers were choked with letters and editorials arguing the contests. The majority of the pieces generally ignored the issues and attacked the character of the candidates. Typically, potential officeholders were accused either of being cheats, slanderers, and liars, or of being unfriendly to democratic principles. Occasionally, at this time of personal politics, a perennial candidate would be accused of sexual misconduct. One lurid story about Ratliff Boon, for example, caused the Warrick County native to announce the charge as absolutely false and accuse a sometimes opponent, Robert Evans, of making up and circulating the fraudulent story to gain political advantage. The wily Evans, in a letter to the *Evansville Gazette*, denied he had given any such report but in doing so cunningly repeated the bawdy tale: "A report is in circulation which I am said to be the author that Col. Boon told me some four or five years ago that he once joined the Baptist church for the sole purpose of seducing a young woman in that church, whom he wished to debauch." Evans then declared, "This statement is incorrect; Col. Boon never made any such statement to me, nor have I made such a statement to any other person."[46]

Ironically, during one of his own political campaigns, Evans himself became embroiled in a ferocious legal battle involving the charge that he had fathered an illegitimate child. For his part, Evans, in a March 17, 1821, issue of the *Indiana Centennial*, did not deny his involvement with "that girl at other times . . . or with any others," adding, "I am not hypocrite enough to pretend to be a saint." Rather, Evans denied he had fathered the child and argued the trial was unfair and carried out by "political enemies to injure me."[47] The political damage wrought by the charge cannot be easily ascertained. Many of Evans's supporters likely understood the entire matter in terms of an attempt to smear an otherwise popular figure. At any rate, Evans lost the election. In 1825 Evans once more ran for the Indiana House. Again, personal politics overrode any other issues. During the campaign, a letter written by Patrick Payne to the editor of the *Gazette* purported to show to what lengths Evans would go to manipulate the outcome of a political contest. "I will state in front of my address," declared Payne, "that General R. M. Evans is a slanderer and not a man of truth." The writer then tells of an earlier election in which Payne had been running for associate judge and Evans spread false charges against Payne concerning the latter's handling an estate. Specifically, Payne accused Evans of treating "voters with

whiskey" on the morning of the election. After getting voters loosened up on "some grog," Evans then "sat down on
the grass and called the attention of the people and cooly
and deliberately made a false charge." Evans responded
quickly and viciously to Payne's charges. In the next issue
of the *Gazette* a letter appeared in which Evans labeled
Payne "a quirking paddy" who had to rely on the testimony
of a "poor little ignorant drunkard" to make his case.[48]
Despite Payne's accusations, Evans won the seat.

When it came to personal politics, Jennings was certainly capable of playing political hardball. In a public letter to his constituents in 1816, Jennings denounced two
pro-Harrison politicians, Evans and William McFarland,
who, "when mustering their field & staff officers mustered
themselves for payment as Colonels in actual service when
28 days of the same time they were actually sitting members of the Territorial Legislature and received their pay
as such; and they severally on the face of their muster
rolls, respectively certify these muster Rolls of their field
& staff, on honour, to be correct." Jennings blasted this
action, declaring, the "conduct on the part of those officers, has been reprobated by every officer of the General
government whose duty it has been to act on those muster
Rolls."[49]

The Jennings faction's distrust of the wily Evans can
also be seen in a letter Nathaniel Ewing sent to Frederick
Rapp, an important member of a large group of recent

immigrants to the state. "I understand Robert M. Evans is also a candidate [for the state constitutional convention]," Ewing wrote. "Beware of him he is verry plausible but no reliance whatever is to be placed on him." Ewing warned Rapp that Evans had "always been opposed to the republicans of the Territory." Worse, the writer declared Evans had "published a verry abusive hand bill agains Mr. Jennings."[50]

Jennings quickly moved to secure jobs for political allies and, in some cases, family members. Jennings offered to procure Mitchell the lucrative job of land registrar at Saint Genevieve in the Missouri Territory.[51] Jesse Holman, John Johnson, and Thomas Scott were all recommended for state supreme court positions. Another example of Jennings's kingdom-building skills at this time involved his relationship with Rapp and the Harmonist colony in the southwest tip of the state. Harmonists had first begun to arrive in Indiana in 1814. The society, since they voted as one under the direction of Rapp, soon became a major political force. In response to this new situation, petitions were sent from one group of the upland southern population in the county to the territorial assembly, complaining that the foreign settlers had "another advantage of our free Citizens by the Right of Suffrage they Vote by advise of their head Mr. Rapp."[52]

Despite the animosity of the original settlers toward the Harmonists, Jennings, always the political realist, quickly moved to secure the support of the Harmonists. In 1817 Jennings traveled to New Harmony to meet with Rapp. A Harmonist letter to Rapp noted, for example, "We had a pleasant visit from Governor Jennings. . . . The Governor expects you in his house upon your return trip."[53] During Jennings's second gubernatorial run, Ewing, a Jennings supporter and business acquaintance of the Harmonists, wrote Rapp informing him of the "great push . . . to get Govr. Jennings turned out & for that purpose [they have] brought forward [Christopher] Harrison and they are making every exertion in their power to have him elected. I have not the least apprehention of his succeeding but I would still be glad how few votes he would get. . . . If you could find it in accord with your Ideas you would confer a perticular obligation on me by giving all the support in your power to Mr. Jennings at the ensuing election."[54]

The Harmonists were producers of several important domestic articles in the region, especially cloth. Jennings shrewdly played on civic pride by ordering cloth for a coat and telling an important Harmonist leader, John Baker, "I have to ask of you the favour to furnish me with a coat pattern of blue cloth (two yards perhaps). When last at Harmony, I was shown some very good cloth at $8 per yd. I wish also a pattern of drab coloured cloth for a great coat, with pretty large cape. If you can have the cloth ready by the next trip which Mr. Bugher will make, and send by him the amount of the cost of the cloth, I will remit you on his return, the money for the same. I want cloth manufactured at Harmony."⁵⁵

A few weeks later Jennings wrote to Rapp, "Your favor of the 18th ult: was received on Wednesday last, together with 2¼ yds. of superfine and 4½ yds. of fine cloth, amounting to forty five dollars. I am much obliged to you for your kind attention, as the cloth is considered to be the best that has been in this place; better even than cloth which has been sold here for $12 and $13 per yard. I shall hereafter endeavour to procure through you, all the cloth which my family may require."⁵⁶ Rapp very much appreciated the governor's attention. In the fall of 1820 he informed Jennings, "It gave us all great pleasure to learn that the first Magistrate of our State shows so much friendship towards domestic manufactores, and condescends to wear some of our cloth. It gave me double satisfaction, Since I waited this long time for an opportunity to show my recognisance towards the many important Services recd. of you, therefore be pleased to accept these few yards of Cloth as a token of my gratitude."⁵⁷ Even toward the end of Jennings's governorship, he continued to order cloth from the Harmonists. In one brief correspondence, he asked that the Harmonists might "be so good as to send me three yards of your best cloth of a blue colour, that you sell for six dollars per yard, if you have not blue send me drab. Six yards of your best white flannel and six of a second quality. I will endeavour to send you the money in a month or two."[58] Again, Rapp made a gift of the order.

Unfortunately, financial problems began to haunt the state and region in Jennings's second term. In a letter printed in the *Corydon Gazette*, Jennings revealed his frustration and concern with the state's dire financial situation. "Various prescriptions," Jennings observed, "have been made by our political doctors to cure the evil. Legislative interferences have been attempted under the confident impression that they would at once remove every difficulty and cause every unfortunate debtor to shake off the shackles of pecuniary oppression. All have proved ineffectual. Still the cloud of adversity thickens. Distress and poverty impudently stare us in the face, as if to proclaim in our very teeth the insufficiency of those measures which have been adopted for their removal."[59] About this same time, Jennings's personal financial problems drove him to cross the line with the Harmonists.

Rapp's followers, through frugal practices and hard work, had weathered the financial crisis rather well. In fact, Rapp had even made a desperately needed loan to the state. In a letter to Rapp in 1822, Jennings requested a personal loan of $1,000:

> Sir, Having understood that you have occasionally loaned money upon interest, allow me to solicit from

you $1,000—or a less sum, for which I will cheerfully pay you 10 per cent, per annum interest on the amount, and repay the principal at any time after a year or 18 months. I will render you secure by leins upon real property or by an assignment of a judgment which I have pending in the Clark Circuit Court, or any other method that will satisfy you. If you can oblige me, it will render me a considerable favour and prevent me from making a sacrafice of some land which has been some time purchased. If you can oblige me, be so good as to inform me by an early reply, and the *terms* when I shall make it my business to visit you at Harmonie.[60]

Jennings's financial difficulties may have been brought on by expenses incurred while serving in political office and by neglect of his farming interests while carrying out political campaigning. Whatever the reason, the Harmonists turned the request down: "In reply to your favor of the 12th inst. I can only say that it has been the Intention and practice of our Society, from its earliest periode, to apply what funds could be spared in making Such improvements as may be requisit for the Comfort and welfare of its members, as well as for the Benefits and convenience of its Neighbours at large. The many exigences of a new Settled and increasing Country dayly call for, and keep pace with our best efforts, Therefore the Society on no instance did or could loan out any money upon Interest whatever, otherwise would cheerfully accommodate you."[61]

Other problems, besides financial ones, also plagued Jennings. One in particular burgeoned into the greatest crisis of his political career. In 1818 Jennings, along with General Lewis Cass of Michigan and Benjamin Parke, received an appointment from President James Madison to be one of the commissioners to negotiate a land purchase with the tribal groups in the central part of the state. Christopher Harrison, a rather eccentric bachelor, had been elected lieutenant governor of Indiana in 1816. Prior to his election, the reclusive Harrison, who came to the territory in 1808, lived alone most of the time in a tiny log cabin on a bluff overlooking the Ohio River. The log cabin was described by one historian as, "but a single room and was roughly made, but inside were many things which testified of the culture of its occupant. Books were there, some of them classical, and paints and brushes and easels were to be seen, and pictures hanging on the wall."[62]

In 1815 the reclusive Harrison moved to Salem, Indiana, where he again lived in semiseclusion. The peculiar Harrison, however, loved flowers and raised them in great profusion in his lot, and children of the village often came to get flowers "and seldom did they go away empty-handed. The master of the house made bouquets and gave them, drew pictures for them, and in many other ways sought to please and make them happy."[63]

Harrison's easy rapport with children, however, did not transfer to his dealings with adults. Before leaving for the treaty meeting, which was in Ohio, the governor, as a matter of practical necessity, sent a memo to his lieutenant governor, casually noting, "that some official business is necessary to be transacted, permit me to inform you that my absence is still necessary, and that it may be necessary for you to attend the seat of government to discharge such duties as devolve on the executive of Indiana."[64] The brief correspondence gave no hint of the storm to follow.

The 1816 Indiana Constitution forbid the holding of any office under either the federal or state government while serving as governor. Further, a state official could not hold "more than one lucrative office at the same time."[65] Perhaps Jennings viewed the Indian negotiations as an essential government service, particularly in light of his unique position as governor of one of the states involved. Or perhaps it was a bit of hubris that caused Jennings to play so loose with the law. It is also unclear whether Harrison's actions were motivated by a desire to uphold legal principle or whether he was encouraged by Jennings's political enemies. At any rate, the event contained many odd twists and turns.

Harrison, upon receiving news that Jennings had left the state, acquired the state seal from Secretary of State New. The lieutenant governor then departed Corydon, leaving the seal, the symbol of executive power, with New. A governor could not endorse official papers without the seal. Harrison had been assured before he left by New that the seal would be surrendered only to him. Things, however, did not work out that way. Upon Harrison's return, he discovered that Jennings had burst into the secretary's office and snatched the seal off a table. Harrison contended that Jennings "had abandoned the office of governor" when he was appointed treaty commissioner and asked for the seal back, but Jennings responded that he would keep it and "be answerable for his own conduct."[66]

Dunn offered a rather dramatic account of the confrontation. When Harrison pointed out that Jennings had forfeited his position, Jennings laughed, pulled out the federal appointment papers and threw them into the fireplace. Jennings then challenged the startled lieutenant governor to prove there was ever a commission.[67] A few years after the incident, Jennings himself explained in a newspaper piece: "With respect to the commission to treat with the Indians, I acted according to my best judgement . . . . As to my monopolizing two offices, and receiving the salaries and emoluments thereof, it is basely false. . . . [Records] show that the Auditor of the state granted a certificate that I neither asked nor received any pay from the state." As for the official commission paper that proved his involvement, Jennings claimed, after the controversy began, that he "destroyed it in disgust."[68]

Whatever the specifics of that first meeting between Harrison and Jennings, Jennings's opponents quickly jumped on the issue. A lengthy letter appeared in the

Jeffersonville Indianian that condemned the governor for knowingly breaking a law. The writer asked, "how far your oath would justify you in exercising two lucrative offices at the same time, and expressly forbidden by the constitution, I know, not, as that is between you and your God. And how far you may think you have claims to merit the people's suffrage, I know not; but think if usurpation, a departure from the constitution, and a corrupt administration will be of any advantage in deciding between merit and demerit, the people will elect some person besides Jonathan Jennings."[69] The most brutal of attacks, however, came from the Vincennes newspaper and its editor, longtime William Henry Harrison supporter Elihu Stout. Stout encouraged unsigned critics to blast away at Jennings. Some of these pieces also brought up a new charge, one that would be repeated many times, of drunkenness. One writer, for example, accused Jennings as being "known and viewed as a drunken sot."[70]

When the Indiana General Assembly met on December 7, 1818, the impasse between the governor and lieutenant governor stood as an emergency situation. The house quickly named a committee to ask Harrison "to communicate . . . the resignation of Jonathan Jennings as Governor . . . and by what way the state seal has been taken out of his [Harrison's] possession." The next day, however, the House realized it might have crossed over its legal bounds and dismissed the committee. Instead, the

House sought Senate consent for a joint committee to call upon both Harrison and Jennings to determine "the true situation of the office of the Executive."[71] The plot thickened when the Senate refused the request. Unable to gain Senate cooperation, the House conceded, by a close vote, to create a joint committee and invite Jennings to explain his side of the story. That same afternoon, Jennings presented his annual governor's address to the legislature. The event yielded at least a symbolic recognition that he was still chief executive. Perhaps Jennings was offering an olive branch to the legislature when he closed the speech by saying, "You have the assurance of my cooperation in every object calculated to promote the prosperity of the state and the happiness of its citizens."[72]

Regardless of the speech, the House continued to inquire into the dispute, again asking both men to report about the situation. The day after Jennings faced the assembly and gave his annual report, the senate proposed a joint committee "to wait on the Lieutenant and late acting Governor." The House agreed with this proposal, but Harrison responded, "That as Lieutenant Governor he had no communication to make . . . but as Lieutenant and acting Governor, if recognized as such, he had."[73] Harrison's uncompromising position caused the joint committee to disband its probe.

The House committee continued investigating, suggesting this body contained the majority of anti-Jennings representatives. Finally, however, by a fifteen to thirteen vote, the House terminated its probe without making a recommendation. Jennings had weathered the storm. Harrison resigned as lieutenant governor, sending a harsh note to the president of the Senate: "As the officers in the executive department of government and the General Assembly of this state have refused to recognize and acknowledge that authority which, according to my understanding, is constitutionally attached to the office, the name itself, in my estimation, is no longer worth retaining."[74] Harrison quickly geared up for a run at the governor's position in the next election. Harrison wagered that the recent furor had generated enough bad feelings toward Jennings to make the governor vulnerable.

Before Jennings's second run for governor, he wrote Holman, telling him his side of the Harrison story: "The House after spending several days on the subject indefinitely postponed it. Since when several seem very anxious to fix on a candidate that may out poll me next august, and talk as if desirous of having a *caucus* for that purpose. The Senate had nothing to do in the whole transaction, at least by any act which appears on the record of their proceedings." Jennings then brought up his real concern. "Those who are most desirous of affecting me urge the idea of bringing you forward as a candidate for the Office of Governor at next election," he said. "What I have given you is the substance of what has transpired here, except what the publick papers will give you. I have delayed writing until the 'Govenor question' was decided and delayed also until nearly the hour of the mail."[75]

Holman did not run, leaving Harrison as Jennings's opponent. Heading the list of charges leveled against Jennings during the campaign was his supposed misuse of office when he served on the Indian treaty commission. However, another cunning Indiana politician, John Tipton, observed, "allegations against Governor Jennings, for Serving his Country as a commissioner in the purchase of the Indian Lands, will have a very different affect from what his enemies intended."[76] Jonathan Woodbury agreed with Tipton's assessment, observing, "As it respects the pending Election for Governor, there is not a Shadow of a doubt against Our friend Jennings Election."[77] Tipton and Woodbury's view turned out to be a correct one. The anti-Jennings forces had more than that one issue. On the eve of the election, a newspaper piece declared that if the people "want a notorious drunkard, then it is proper to vote for Jonathan Jennings."[78] Another article hinted at Jennings's drinking problem by claiming he had been "indisposed" for "a number of days" while serving as treaty commissioner.[79] In a lengthy poem in the *Western Sun*, Jennings was accused of "sipping deep the noxious juice of corn distilled,/or wheat or rye or if per chance/ his heart expands, or others fill/ the cheering bowl, with rosy wine/ he dies away in stupid gloom."[80] These several references

to a drinking problem, while coming from Jennings's enemies, must be considered as having some basis in fact,
given their numbers.

Appealing to voters to throw out "ungodly" political
leaders is not a new practice. The *Western Sun* made just
such a suggestion regarding Jennings during his second
run for office: "Remember the love you bear your wives
and children, whom you have promised to nourish and
protect, your duty to yourselves and to your country, and I
may add, the solemn debt of gratitude you owe the
Supreme Being . . . and surely you will come forward . . .
and put an end to the reign of wickedness and folly."[81]
Regardless of this and other attacks, Jennings defeated
Harrison by almost a three-to-one margin. Carmony
assessed this triumph as coming "in part because of the
popularity he had achieved since his election as a territorial delegate a decade earlier."[82] Cayton observed that
Jennings became a target "of the same kind of charges of
aristocracy which they had leveled at Harrison. . . . Many
citizens of the new state seemed to believe by the 1820s
that they had merely exchanged one oligarchy for
another."[83] Jennings had obviously built a political apparatus of his own.

Jennings's Pennsylvania cultural background can be
seen coming out in his early support of education during
his service as governor. Many of the upland South settlers
who now served in positions of state leadership did not

value or support public education. Even by the late 1830s, Fletcher often complained in his diary of the anti-education attitude of the majority of Hoosiers. Regarding the maintenance of public education in the state, Fletcher wrote, "Not one leading politician, not one newspaper press in the state dare lift its head in its behalf."[84] Indeed, Indiana lingered far behind other midwestern states for decades in terms of advancing public education.[85] But Jennings understood the value of this commodity, and in his 1817 annual message to the state legislature declared, "the establishment of a system of common schools throughout the inhabited portion of our state" to be of upmost importance. "The operation of such a system," Jennings pointed out, "so arranged as to afford the means of every description of our citizens to educate their children, will secure the morals of the rising generation, the better prepare them for the discharge of their several . . . duties."[86] Unfortunately, Jennings's vision regarding education did not resonate among most Hoosiers.

Jennings's service as governor was not without humorous moments. In one example, Jennings, in a letter to U.S. Secretary of State John C. Calhoun requesting three large cannons for the state, wrote a short, witty poem:

> Dear good John C.
> I send to thee
> For three great guns and trimmings,

Pray send them to hand,
Or You'll be damned.
By order of Jonathan Jennings.[87]

Jennings was prohibited by law from running for a third term as governor in 1823. Jennings's reign as Indiana's first chief executive secured him a place in the state's history. The office, however, was greatly limited, and Jennings accomplished very little other than serving as a sort of caretaker of the state. Jennings's own assessment of the office was harsh and to the point. To Mitchell, he confided, "I hold an office, considered honorable, but I know it to be capable of yielding but little satisfaction."[88]

8

"Throwed by as useless"

AT THE END OF HIS FINAL TERM AS GOVERNOR, JONATHAN Jennings realized he wanted to continue his political career, despite his oft-stated longing to retire to a cabin in the Indiana woods. It was unlikely that Jennings, at thirty-eight years of age, would be willing or able to depend on the harsh and difficult life of farming as his only livelihood. In addition, the economic situation in the state and the nation made agricultural efforts especially difficult, as evidenced by Jennings's attempt to borrow money from the Harmonists. Jennings at this point also maintained a strong grasp on his political machine. Many historians, based on the opinion of Indiana politician Oliver H. Smith in 1858, believed that Jennings worked out an arrangement with other politicians to exchange offices. According to Smith, "affairs of the State were then in the hands of three parties, or rather one party with three divisions—the Noble, Jennings and Hendricks divisions—which were all

fully represented in the convention that formed the constitution of 1816. . . . It was evident to these leaders that
personal political conflicts must arise between them
unless the proper arrangements were made to avoid them.
It was then agreed between them to aid each other in
making [James] Noble United States Senator, Jennings
Governor, and [William] Hendricks Congressman."[1] While
historians have debated the strength of this connection and
the amount of actual cooperation among the three men, it
is likely that Hendricks and Jennings had links through
their Pennsylvania background and that Jennings had
showed Hendricks favor at the 1816 convention.

This 1822 episode of political musical chairs played
out in an unusual fashion. Hendricks resigned his seat in
Congress to run for governor, and Jennings ran to fill the
vacant congressional position while still in the governor's
chair. More confusing to the voters, Jennings's campaign
involved a run for the vacant seat of Hendricks as well as
a seat for the next full term. To make matters more complex, the full-term slot would be for one of Indiana's three
new districts, while the position Hendricks had held represented the entire state. Jennings attempted to explain
the complication to voters in a letter to his constituents:
"My object in this address is to prevent my views from
being mis-represented, as well as to prevent any deception
from being practiced upon those who have not made the
subject of the approaching election an object of enquiry."

Jennings went on to note, "To prevent any confusion growing out of the circumstances of both elections taking place
on the first Monday of August next, it is only necessary for
the voter to give in a ticket he may wish as his representative next winter . . . and another ticket for the person whom
he wishes to represent him winter after next."[2]

Jennings's political foe for the vacant seat was Davis
Floyd, while Judge James Scott opposed him for one of
the three new congressional seats. The campaign carried
all the intensity of the other campaigns in which Jennings
had labored. The most perilous problem for Jennings
emerged in a newspaper article in the *Madison Western
Clarion*, in which Jennings was confronted by ten questions, including one that asked, "Why did Jonathan
Jennings wish to 'monopolize' the seats of Indiana government? Had he not already served as governor and territorial delegate to Congress?" Perhaps the most interesting
one was the last question, which inquired, "How had
Governor Jennings spent the day he set aside by proclamation for fasting and prayer? Had he refused to participate in 'pious acts of devotion?' Had he not spent the day
sleeping late in a private home after a night in
Charlestown 'public house' practicing the 'vice of drinking
and card playing?'"[3] The article was printed on handbills
and distributed throughout Indiana.

Typically, handbills such as this were passed out in a
way to keep the accused from having time to respond.

Fortunately, Jennings found out about the article and handbills in time to answer his adversaries. To David Mitchell he wrote, "[John] Ross set off to Salem and there published the abusive questions against me and if I had not happened to be at Charleston I should not have had it in my power to answer in any time to reach the people. He would not publish at Charleston. [W]hen if I had remained at Corydon I should not have seen them until this evening." Regarding his response, Jennings noted, "You will [see] the questions in the Madison papers, but I send you this lest they, as papers might not arrive. I think they had better (the questions and answers) be published. I sent to you a number of Handbills. I wish you to enquire at the printing office for them and be particular to address them on the back to particular individuals not forgetting the proper persons in town."[4]

In a second letter to Mitchell, Jennings complained, "I am do[ing] pretty well, but they are making great exertions. Ross went from Charleston to Salem and published those interrogatories, sent them to Charleston and Madison to be republished and he Ross made himself responsible for payment, expecting that I would not see them in time to answer, at least soon enough to circulate them, but I have made great exertion and succe[ss]fully." Jennings ended by hoping "my friends will attend to Harrison and Crawford Counties. I sent through Col. Ranney to you or to the Post office a number of Handbills to be distributed in Harrison and Clark Counties. I hope that my friends will attend to the management of my enemies in Crawford & Harrison Counties."[5] In yet another note to Mitchell he begged, "Some of my friends must keep a good look out. Could not some one go to Crawford [County]."[6]

Jennings's responses to the ten questions apparently worked wonders. He began his response by noting the political timing of the charges: "I pledge myself to my fellow citizens to make appear in due time, and at a more proper season than is selected to attack me." Jennings further pointed out that almost all of the accusations were old charges and had already been hashed out. "The questions which are put to me for answers, are connected with transactions, some of which transpired nearly twelve years ago, and all except three of them have been passed upon by my fellow citizens by large majorities in my favor," he asserted. But Jennings's response to the accusations of gambling and drinking are interesting, given that other drinking charges had recently surfaced: "It is false and infamously false. I gambled not, nor was I intoxicated." Jennings then explained that while he was "not a professor of religion," the accusations were false and raised to do political harm.[7]

The statewide race to fill the vacancy left by Hendricks was apparently of great concern to the Jennings organization. John D. Hay wrote to Harmonist leader Frederick Rapp to express worry over rumors that Jennings was "loosing ground fast" and that "Floyd will out run him on the general ticket."[8] Jennings, however, gained a broad victory, winning the statewide race over Floyd by a wide margin and defeating Scott by 1,373 votes for the second district seat in the eighteenth Congress.[9]

By late 1822 Jennings found himself back in Washington, D.C., complaining once more of the political goings-on there. To Samuel Milroy he wrote, "We have here a great field of intrigue and arrangements . . . certain men of certain views look with a very jealous eye upon any proposition which touches the Public Lands or the completion of our great Western national road; more so than I could have believed before I witnessed it." Jennings himself wished to see "Domestic manufacturers flourish and internal improvement progress as fast as these objects can be accomplished without a resort to internal tax."[10] Jennings's opinion regarding government help for internal improvements was not universally shared. Englishwoman Frances Trollope observed House debates during this time and told of witnessing "the very singular effect of . . . man after man start eagerly to his feet, to declare that the greatest injury, the basest injustice, the most obnoxious tyranny that could be practised against the state of which he was a member, would be a vote of a few million dollars for the purpose of making their roads or canals; or for drainage; or in short, for any purpose of improvement whatsoever."[11]

Trollope also noted a number of interesting features of the capital in the 1820s. Of debates in the House, Trollope observed that she "could only follow one or two of the orators, whose voices were peculiarly loud and clear. This made it really a labour to listen; but the extreme beauty of the chamber was of itself a reason for going again and again. It was, however, really mortifying to see this splendid hall, fitted up in so stately and sumptuous a manner, filled with men, sitting in the most unseemly attitudes, a large majority with their hats on, and nearly all, spitting to an excess that decency forbids me to describe."[12] Of the use of tobacco, as well as the overall general posture of the representatives, Trollope commented, "The spitting was incessant; and not one in ten of the male part of the illustrious legislative audience sat according to the usual custom of human beings; the legs were thrown sometimes over the front of the box, sometimes over the side of it; here and there a senator stretched his entire length along a bench, and in many instances the front rail was preferred as a seat."[13]

Frederick Marryat, another visitor, observed a darker presence than tobacco. Explaining that alcohol was forbidden, Marryat observed, "I wondered how the members could get on without [alcohol], but upon this point I was soon enlightened. Below the basement of the building is an oyster-shop and refectory. The refectory has been permitted by Congress upon the express stipulation that no spirituous liquors should be sold there, but law-makers are too often law-breakers all over the world. You go there and ask for a pale sherry, and they hand you gin; brown sherry, and it is brandy; madeira, whiskey; and thus do these potent, grave, and reverend signors evade their own laws, beneath the very hall wherein they were passed in solemn conclave."[14] Sadly, as Jennings's time in the capital passed, the amount of time he spent in local drinking places like the one Marryat described increased.

In the early part of his term, Jennings cemented a key political alliance back in Indiana. John Tipton, an upland southerner, had migrated to the Corydon area in 1807. Records indicate Jennings had appointed Tipton to several important posts (sheriff, brigade general, and major general of the militia). He and Jennings may have grown particularly close after Jennings selected him in 1820 as one of the commissioners to select the site of the new state capital.[15] The men would have also have known each other through their Masonic work, an important political networking tool in early Indiana politics.[16]

In 1825 Jennings secured an especially lucrative position for Tipton as Indian agent at Fort Wayne. The job was a powerful political tool that gave Tipton opportunities to pass profitable treaty and trading appointments on to friends and would-be allies. They, in turn, would most likely have been politically loyal to Tipton's mentor, Jennings. For his part, Jennings clearly protected this investment. He quickly communicated with John C. Calhoun on Tipton's behalf following Tipton's confiscation of the goods of the American Fur Company after its agents sold liquor illegally to the Indians. "My friend Gen. John Tipton of Fort Wayne," Jennings wrote, "informs me that in consequence of seizures made by him as Indian Agent; he is informed that exertions are to be made to his injury. . . . So far as is proper, I should be glad to be informed of what is doing and by whom; at least if any representations shall be made touching his [Tipton's] integrity."[17] The Tipton/Jennings friendship was apparently recognized throughout the state. One would-be appointee, for example, mentioned to Tipton, "I know the influence you have with [Jennings] and his disposition to oblige you."[18] In 1826 Jennings helped Tipton secure a commissioner seat to an Indian treaty, another profitable endeavor. In their most important bonding experience, Jennings fought hard to protect his friend from charges brought against him while he served as Indian agent. Tipton repaid his friend Jennings in a most generous and loyal fashion.

An ambitious and restless man such as Jennings could not have stayed happy as a representative for long. Having served in that capacity a number of times, and as the state's first governor, it was only natural he would come to set his sights on a U.S. Senate term. Hendricks, a sometime ally, stood as Jennings's most immediate foe for a seat in 1825. At the time, the Indiana House elected U.S.

Senators. In a letter to Mitchell, Jennings shrewdly observed, "I find in the Eastern part of the state, that if Hendricks were out of the way, my election would be almost certain." Jennings then asked his brother-in-law to find out what Hendricks "is doing and what does he intend to do. Deal with him quite *mildly* and let me hear from you without delay, embracing such view as may be useful to me." Jennings then pondered his future political possibilities in terms of a senate run: "Some certain gentlemen, in the East, talk of my residence as being not sufficiently West, and attempts will therefore be made to unite, in political concert the East and West part of the State. This is to be guarded against prudently, but I believe a majority of the Eastern members will not join in such course however they may vote. Clay has the vote of this state by a majority of nearly 700 votes. Do let me hear from you without delay. Tell me all; and what the Governor says about '*not being a candidate if I am.*'" Jennings also brought up another problem which would grow in time, that of his health. He told Mitchell of "Rheumatism in my knees—not much pain but stiff and sore when [I] get up from a chair or sit down; can walk when on foot pretty [well] and ride when mounted."[19] As for the Senate election, on the first ballot, Isaac Blackford received twenty-six votes, Hendricks twenty-five, and Jennings ten. On the fourth ballot, Hendricks was elected by a vote of thirty-two to thirty over Blackford.[20]

In the midst of the sting of this first defeat, Jennings found himself facing a much more distressing event: the increasing illness of his wife Ann Hay Jennings. To his friend John Graham Jennings wrote in 1825, "Mrs. J. is still confined to bed [but] has gained I think, a small accession of strength and her stomach is not so subject to sickness and cascading as it was two or three months since."[21] Interestingly, accounts affording insights into Jennings's feelings toward his wife as time passed can not be found, if they exist at all. He simply seemed to mention his "little Ann" less and less except for brief comments about her illnesses. The couple had no children, although they took in Ebenezer Jennings's son for a brief time. Jacob Jennings later graduated from Washington College in Pennsylvania. Jacob's sister, Maria, was taken in by Ann and David Mitchell.[22]

Jennings himself suffered health problems in Washington while Ann grew weaker in Indiana. In a letter to his constituents in 1824, a frustrated Jennings reported, "I have been severely afflicted with a violent attack of a bilious rheumatism, of which however, I am recovering, but which has disenabled me for a considerable time to attend to business, and even yet I write with pain, owing to the effect which the rheumatism has left upon my arms and shoulders. I hope soon to be able however to write with less difficulty, when I shall submit to you my views in relation to such subjects as have been under the deliberation of congress, and calculated from their character to claim an interest in your attention."[23]

In January 1826 Ann's deteriorating health caused Jennings to explain to a friend that while he struggled in the House of Representatives to relieve Hoosiers who suffered under heavy debt, his mind stayed preoccupied with worry about his wife's illness. He had good cause for concern. Ann died at her brother's residence in March 1826. She was thirty-four years of age. A grieving Jennings wrote David Mitchell two months later, lamenting, "I have suffered, not a little this winter." At the top of his list of sad events was "the death of my wife in my absence."[24] Less than a year later, Jennings's beloved childhood friend and sister, Ann Mitchell, died. Jennings wrote his grieving brother-in-law, telling him, "Your letter of the 24th of last month did not reach me until this morning. The tidings it brings is painful enough though not altogether unexpected. I expect she is now happy, and this is the only consolation left to you and her friends. Indeed I have no doubt of it. I deeply condole with you and sincerely agree with you that religion is no chimera, and wish that I were a subject of its influence. I still hope to be. I should have been greatly gratified if I could have been near my dear Sister. But never more in this world."[25]

Despite the sorrows, Jennings still possessed political aspiration. He made a second run at a U.S. Senate seat and also considered running again for Indiana governor.

Regarding the latter possibility, Jordan Vigus, a political dabbler of sorts, explained to Tipton in 1827, "Mr. Jennings is here & is warmley solisited to becum a candidate for Govirner the south & the west will Suport him through out I beleave."[26] Not all astute Hoosier politicians saw Jennings's future as particularly bright. Calvin Fletcher informed Tipton that, in his opinion, Jennings had been knocked "on the ground" because of one of his House votes and suggested that Jennings might indeed run for the more certain position of governor.[27] Apparently, by this time, Hendricks had turned on his old political ally, as he too sought a coveted Senate seat. Sam Milroy explained to Tipton, "Mr. Hendrick . . . is an administration man undisguised—interested in our canal and Michigan road & I consider him a faithful man, to the intrest of Indiana, tho I cannot aprove his oposition to our old friend Jennings."[28]

Fate, which smiled upon Jennings in the past, now seemed to turn its head. Illness, alcohol abuse, and a changing political landscape all worked against his ambitions. The appearance of Andrew Jackson on the political scene had resurrected political parties, and the age of personal politics, an arena in which Jennings had shined, had begun to fade. Jackson, the hero of the Battle of New Orleans during the War of 1812, was immensely popular among Hoosiers. Adam Leonard, an early Indiana historian, noted of this phenomenon, "Jacksonian democracy . . .

was the manifest expression of that intense feeling that the common man was supreme."[29] The presidential election of 1824, pitting Jackson, John Quincy Adams, and Henry Clay against one another, dawned as a historic event for Hoosiers. The election witnessed the first time political parties organized and opposed one another. It was also a crucial time for Jennings, who tended to favor the ideas of Adams and later those of Clay, especially regarding the support of internal improvements. However, Jennings's keen political instincts caused him to lean toward Jackson publicly.

After the dust of the 1824 national election had settled, Jackson held a large lead in the popular vote. The electoral votes, however, had been split three ways, causing the election to be thrown into the House of Representatives. Aware the popular opinion within the state favored Jackson, Jennings and the two other congressmen from the Hoosier State voted accordingly. Consequently, despite his personal support of the Adams ticket, Jennings, as he often did, gave way to political reality. Jackson, however, was ultimately defeated in the House by a deal between the two other candidates. Adams became president, and Clay became his secretary of state. This left Hoosier supporters of Jackson extraordinarily energized for the next election.

Perhaps the strangest episode of Jennings's political career occurred during his second attempt to gain a senate

seat. As Jackson's star rose on the frontier, the main oppos-
ing force, under the national leadership of Adams and Clay,
chose William Henry Harrison to travel to Indiana and
rally their supporters. Still enamored with the hero of
Tippecanoe, Hoosier crowds converged on the former territorial governor when he came to Vincennes in 1826.
Jennings joined Harrison on the stump. The two old foes
found themselves serving on the same side and understood
that politics required they present a front of reconciliation.
Jennings reported, in a letter to Clay, that he had cautioned
his former political enemy to not bring up their old rivalry
as it could hinder Jennings in his quest for the senate.
Harrison, as reported to Clay, also informed Jennings he
would not interfere in the election so as to let state political forces play out.[30]

If Jennings had hoped for a direct endorsement from
Harrison, he was disappointed. In his speech Harrison
mentioned, perhaps with a brief glance in Jennings's direction, that he had come to the fledgling territory in 1800
"young and inexperienced and clothed with a power unsur-
passed in the country which ought never to be confided to
any individual." Harrison's dictatorial powers while serving
as territorial governor had been the cornerstone of
Jennings's many bitter attacks against Harrison in the earlier days of both men's careers. Wisely, Harrison moved
to a friendlier subject. The former governor emphasized
the Battle of Tippecanoe and applauded the people of

William Henry Harrison in his later years.

Vincennes for their courage during the Indian dangers. Harrison ended his talk by toasting Jennings for his "long and faithful service as first governor."[31]

The thirty-four-year-old Jennings calmly stood up and made a short speech. Among a few other points, Jennings pondered a mystery that had long fascinated him: one's destiny. Of this matter, Jennings offered, "Fate makes some men, and some men make their fate—it was [my] fate to be placed in the office of governor of this state; and [I] could assure [my] citizens, that [I] entered upon the discharge of its duties with an unqualified determination to promote the best interests of the state, so far as [I] should find [myself] competent."[32]

Everything seemed to go smoothly at Vincennes. If anyone caught the irony of the whole event, that of once-fierce enemies working together, nothing officially was noted. In private, however, Harrison confided to Clay that he "could take no part whatever in the contest. Jennings told me he was certain that I would do him no injury & that his only wish was to be upon an equal footing with the others by letting the people know that We Were no longer enemies."[33] The political troupe, Harrison, Blackford, and Jennings, left Vincennes and traveled to Princeton. Here once more Jennings found himself toasted at the main dinner.[34] After the two visits to Indiana, Harrison shared his own calculations with Clay as to the senate race outcome: "The rival candidates for the Senate in Indiana have

been very active Blackford & Jennings Were with me at
Vincennes & Princeton. The former will get the members
from the West end of the State with the exception of one
or two & those will be in favor of Noble. The center
Districts are generally for Jennings But there also Noble
will break in upon him. I think upon the whole that
Nobles prospects are best But the friends of Blackford calculate with some prospect of success of getting the Votes
of Jennings ulimately."[35] Harrison was correct; Noble won
the senate seat for in spite of Jennings's well-organized
campaign.

In his last term as representative, Jennings continued
to champion internal improvements, proudly explaining to
citizens in his district, "Thus far Indiana has obtained, a
much greater proportion of the public resources, in com-
parison to her population, than a large majority of the
other states of the Union. Decidedly in favor of internal
improvement myself, yet some settled system should be
adopted, calculated to do equal justice, or we may have . . .
conflicts and jealousies among the states, calculated to
retard a regular progress of the work, and operate most
injuriously to the harmony and unison of action which
should be cherished, each towards each other, by the
states of the Union."[36] Jennings also stayed in close contact
with Tipton, a rising star in Hoosier politics. In one interesting letter, Jennings offered his own view of the state's
political landscape:

I now detail to you what I give to your confidence and alone to your confidence. Soon after the Supreme Court in May last, I was asked if I knew of any measures in contemplation to defeat Hendricks in the next election to the Senate, and whether I thought of being a candidate. To this I replied I knew of none, and as to myself I had neither written nor made any calculations of being a candidate nor did I intend so to do. I was then asked, if I knew whether you did not intend to be a candidate. I replied that I had no information on that subject whatever. Just before Mr. Gray left here for your Town, I was told that Sweetzer said to Howk, that he wanted to put Hendricks down. Howk has long disliked Hendricks. Howk replied by assenting, if he could elect in the place of Hendricks some person to please him, and named me. Sweetzer observed I would not do—that the same objection lay to me as to Hendricks, viz, we were not Jackson-men, and it must be a Jackson man, who with some votes from members of the Legislature that were Adams men would defeat Hendricks. . . . Appearances would indicate, that Noble intends to give Hendricks a back-handed blow.[37]

Of his own political future, Jennings remarked to Tipton, "I have no desire but to remain for a time in my present station, and rid myself of pecuniary obligations as soon as I can."[38] This sudden lack of interest in politics may have been driven by growing financial concerns. As early as 1823 Jennings was no longer in a position to loan money to his close friend John Graham, although he had cheerfully done so in the past. "Such is my situation," he reported to Graham, "that I am entirely unable to oblige you. Coopers disappointments have given me much difficulty and I am expecting a draft upon me after a few days, that will be as much as I can meet & indeed before long and before summer I shall be on the borrowing list, unless Cooper shall do something for me. I am sorry it is not in my [power] to oblige you, but so it is."[39] By the late 1820s Jennings's financial situation had grown precarious. In 1829 he wrote Tipton, telling him, "I cannot visit you this year. I am making arrangements to move into the country and moreover am short of spare cash, having unexpectedly to meet $400—which I had borrowed from Doc. Hay two years ago."[40] The wear and tear of political life that Jennings endured is revealed in a letter Tipton wrote to a friend, George Spencer, in 1829: "I have been long in the public service [and] am wearied of *turmoil, bustle*—and *censures* think I will resign (if not remooved) in about one year from December next. my head is grown gray in the service of my country . . . I am admonished by every day that I live of the necessity of taking time, *between public life* and *death* for for *sober thinking*."[41]

But Jennings could not afford to abandon politics. Indeed, Jennings had become a professional officeholder, depending on the money the position paid to take care of his life's expenses. Still, by the mid-1820s, it was barely enough. Jennings's poor financial circumstances were further exacerbated by a freak accident at his Washington residence. In January 1827, as he sat before the fireplace in his chamber at Queens Hotel, "a quantity of plastering fell on his head." One account said he was "much injured" in the occurrence.[42] The next July he informed his constituents that health issues would limit his direct interaction with those he represented. "The excessive heat, the length of the journey and my yet limited strength," he informed citizens of the Second Congressional District, "will render my travel tedious, and deprive me, therefore, of visiting but a very small portion of the district."[43] One positive event did occur for Jennings at this time. In October 1827 he married Clarissa Barbee of Kentucky. Whatever newfound happiness the union brought to Jennings, it was not, however, sufficient to overcome his growing addiction to alcohol. House journals concerning Jennings's last term indicate he did little work, a circumstance that may have been caused by his increased drinking.

In the nineteenth century, alcoholism was not considered a disease. In fact, the prevalence of drinking seemed to reach an all-time high in Jennings's day.[44] Social historian W. J. Rorabaugh noted, for example, that at this time, "Americans drank on all occasions. Every social event demanded a drink." Alcohol became a familiar item at Hoosier public events such as militia musters, elections, and the quarterly sessions of courts. Furthermore, westerners in states such as Indiana believed that whiskey was healthful "because it was made of a nutritive grain, that it was patriotic to drink it because corn was native, and that it's wholesome."[45]

In Indiana, alcohol abuse was especially disturbing. The Hoosier frontier witnessed hardworking, often lonely men and women living and toiling under adverse conditions. They were also often ignorant of the long-range consequences of some of their lifestyle choices. Many found that alcohol, especially homemade whiskey, brought some relief from the harshness of frontier life. One Vanderburgh County, Indiana, pioneer recorded that weary ministers often arrived at a house to conduct religious services and used whiskey as a stimulant. Whiskey, the settler further reported, sold for five cents a glass, while fifteen cents would buy a small jugful.[46] The popularity of whiskey on the raw frontier was powerfully described by William W. Sweet, who noted it was considered as much a necessity as bread and meat. "Everybody indulged—men, women, and children, preachers, and church members, as well as the ungodly," Sweet noted. "Stores had open kegs of whiskey with cups attached for all to help themselves. It was freely served in all the social gatherings, log rollings, corn huskings, and house raisings."[47] It is not surprising, then, that many early settlers soon found themselves engaged in an impossible struggle with alcohol.

Baptists were especially known for their consumption of alcohol. Their early reputation earned them the name of Forty-Gallon Baptists. Posey County, Indiana, records reveal, for example, that early Baptist ministers often sold liquor. In 1817 Thomas Givens, a prominent Baptist of the regular, Calvinistic body, was "allowed a license to keep a house of public entertainment" where alcohol was served. The most prominent Baptist minister of the area, Samuel Jones, also owned a tavern. Joshua Elkins, a Baptist layman who ran afoul of the law in 1813 for selling whiskey without a license, paid the sum of four dollars as a county tax on his tavern in 1817.[48]

Unfortunately for Jennings, drinking also had long been at the heart of frontier politics. Calvin Fletcher told of one typical Hoosier election day where the candidates and voters "took brandy which soon produced intoxication."[49] Another witness reported an election day in the Northwest Territory: "The stump speeches being over, then commenced the drinking of liquor, and long before night a large portion of the voters [were] drunk and staggering about town, cursing, swearing hallooing, yelling, huzzaing, for their favorite candidates."[50] An editorial in one 1821 Indiana newspaper complained after one election, "We were mortified to hear some severe censure on the immoderate use of whiskey. . . . Surely candidates for office would not wish to have it understood that their popularity rest upon the strength of whiskey."[51] This editorial, however, was especially optimistic for frontier Indiana.

By the early 1830s a strong temperance movement began to emerge at both the national and state levels, and Jennings, at the strong insistence of his friends, took a pledge to stop drinking. But the promise failed. It would be many years later that Bill Wilson would come to understand that an alcoholic could usually not imagine never drinking again. Many could, however, think in terms of sobriety for a twenty-four hour period. The one-day-at-a-time philosophy became the cornerstone of what would become Alcoholics Anonymous.[52] Using a twelve-step program, AA has been a tool of recovery that has produced significant results, as have other recovery programs that use a medical model as a way of dealing with the disease. Still, with its tremendous desire to drink, the disease does not go away but, at best, stays in remission. Frederick Kitner wrote Tipton of Jennings's apparent attempt at keeping a temperance pledge, noting sarcastically, "As it regards my stating on paper that I never again would taste spiritous liquors, I would only ask you to refer to the letter of Mr. Jennings on the subject, and see in what a situation he has placed himself in toward you."[53]

In 1831 John Carr, a political friend of Jennings, wrote Tipton of his concern for Jennings's heavy drinking. "If our friend Jonathan Jennings does not reform his habits, he will be dissuaded from becoming a candidate for Congress at the election in 1831," Carr warned. Carr also mentioned that many concerned voters had asked him to run for

Jennings's seat, but Carr, because of his friendship with Jennings, claimed having "no particular solitude to enter."[54] But Jennings's drinking had created such a political liability that Carr eventually did run for the seat and in a six-way race badly defeated Jennings, who came in a distant third. After the election, a guilt-ridden Carr explained to Tipton, "It was with reluctance that I did consent to be run in opposition to Mr. Jennings." Surprisingly, Jennings still held some hope for a U.S. Senate seat. Carr explained the political situation as it stood for their friend: "A great deal is said about the Election for Senator in congress. Messrs Jennings [Samuel] Judah and yourself are spoken of as the Jackson candidates in this quarter and [there is] diversity of opinion in relation to the strength of each. Sympathy will do much for Mr. Jennings." Perhaps, after witnessing how Jennings's seeming reputation as an alcoholic had affected the last election, Carr added, "But I am doubtful he cannot be sustained."[55]

Carr's observation proved correct. Jennings's hope for the Senate soon faded. The once-premier Hoosier politician now found himself without a public office. To make matters worse, prospects in Indiana for a successful life outside politics were bleak. Once home from Washington, Jennings wrote to a friend, "I reached my Cabin in safety, though quite a disagreeable travel. My home business, Mills & Co., not doing well; and [I] have been necessarily much engaged."[56]

Retirement from public office did little to help Jennings with his drinking. The former governor traveled frequently on his horse into Charlestown to visit the local tavern. One account claimed that an intoxicated Jennings would mount his faithful horse and depend on it to get him safely home when its rider was in a highly intoxicated state. Occasionally, Jennings fell from his mount and lay in the street or crawled to the relative safety of the roadside, where he lay in a stupor. Once two travelers trekking through Charlestown spied Jennings leaning drunk against a tree. One recognized the pathetic figure and explained to the other that it was the former governor. Hearing the comment, Jennings slowly raised his head and remarked, "Yes, a pretty governor. He can't govern himself."[57]

Tipton tried one more time to pull his friend from the grip of alcohol and help him financially in the process. The latter situation, a lack of money, loomed as a pressing problem for Jennings. In late 1831 Tipton, as a U.S. senator, possessed the crucial power to choose three representatives from Indiana to help negotiate a treaty with the Native Americans. Political friends bombarded Tipton with pleas to be among the three chosen. Joseph Holman, for example, wrote, "You said when I saw you last something about a treaty in the North—I should like to have a finger in some rich pie."[58] In another letter, Holman noted, "A word for me, from you . . . will be of great service. . . . I would like to furnish the Public Table . . . by which I can make some money."[59] William Wick, another hopeful, wrote Tipton: "Now one word as to my own affairs. There will I suppose be a Treaty with our Indians." Then he proposed, "I want to make $500 somehow or other—by being Secretary to the Commissioners—a contract or any other honorable way. I need the money, and am willing to render faithful service for it. Cannot you smuggle me in as an originell Jackson man or as an 11th hour convert, or as being under serious convictions, or let the rule be waived in my favor a little? I know *your* feelings on these subjects. I have never ate a dinner or drunk a glass of wine at the expense of Uncle Sam's loaves & fishes & just want a little sop now if it be my turn. I want the money to pay my electioneering expences next summer a year."[60]

In a letter to Fletcher, Tipton explained why he picked Jennings for the final slot: "When I wrote to you a few days ago I thought and intended to have your friend [William] Conner appointed. since that the name of my old benefactor Jennings has been presented, not by me but by another. I have wrote for Conner but go for Jennings. both if I can get them but Jenings over every other man on earth."[61] William Polke told Tipton he was "much gratified that Mr. Jennings is one [chosen] and I hope it will yet save him at any Rate we must try to aid him all in our power so that an old and Beneficial public servant may not be throwed by as useless."[62] Apparently, however, Jennings and the other two commissioners failed to gain a treaty. One witness wrote, "the course pursued during the time we were assembled for the purpose of treating was so different from that adopted by the commissioners of the United States on former occasions . . . that the Indians were very much dissatisfied."[63]

Tipton remained loyal to Jennings even when Jennings failed to help secure Tipton's successful re-election to a Senate seat in 1832. William Marshall explained to Tipton how the drama played out: "You will see in the Democrat and Journal of this place The final results of, and may different ballots by the Legislator, for the United States senator. . . . Gov. Jennings arrived here after the battle was over he done his best to get here sooner but failed."[64]

In mid 1832 a financially struggling Jennings asked Tipton and Charles Dewey to buy the title for Jennings's farm. The Jennings/Dewey friendship went back at least to Jennings's second term as governor, as Dewey had been Jennings's counselor during the Christopher Harrison crisis in 1819. Jennings, in turn, had repaid Dewey by recommending him to a judgeship. Dewey relayed his thoughts to Tipton in a letter, which indicates the desperate shape Jennings found himself in by 1832:

Mr. Jennings has requested me to state to you my opinion respecting the title to his farm. This request he made, as I understand him, in consequence of a letter from you to *Ferguson*. His title to the farm is encumbered by two mortgages—one to a Mr. Stephens—and the other to Jacob Jennings now deceased. The Stephens mortgage, though of later date than the other, is the prior lien, in consequence of its being first recorded. An assignment by Stephens to you of its debt against Mr. Jennings together with the mortgage, will place you in his stead, and give you the oldest lien upon the property— Jennings' mortgage cannot affect the land until the other is paid off. This the holder of that mortgage has a right to do. And probably he has also a right to procure a decree of event, that the land be sold first to discharge Stephens' mortgage, and then his own. The Stephens mortgage was originally for $800—the other for $1000. I do not know what is due on either . . . Be this, however, as it may, I believe, that the purchase of the Stephens Mortgage would be a safe transaction to the purchaser.[65]

Tipton agreed to take on the burden, telling businessman and banker James Lanier, "In reply to your letter of the 20 Inst informing me that mr Jenings land was sold and could be redeemed I send you my check for $200 and enclose you a letter from Govr Jenings wrote before he had seen or heard from you save his farm with as little loss as possible to me. I am hard pressed for cash cannot conveniently raise more than $1000 but if Stevens or Dewey presses I will try to raise more rather than see J[onathan] J[ennings] turned out of doors. will leave this matter wholly to your discretion."[66]

By 1834 this commitment put a great burden upon Tipton, who complained to Lanier he could not purchase any insurance stock Lanier had suggested as a good buy because he was "hard presed for cash." Tipton further complained to his friend, "The purchase of the Jenings property will keep me so for a year."[67] Perhaps fearing Jennings's diminished capacity at this time due to his drinking, and wanting at the same time to recoup some of the investment, Tipton, in another letter, told Lanier, "I hold all the papers in relation to the Jennings land and had better do so until a final close of the matter—I gave Dewey a paper in your name signifying that you would permit Jennings to remain on the premises during his natural life he to pay all taxes and not to destroy timber. It must not be known that Jennings has a legal right to possession during life–(indeed J. does not himself know that he has a legal right, he supposes he is dependent entirely on your pleasure) as this right can be sold under an Exn. in mentioning the subject you had better say that you *intend to permit* him to remain. The time is coming when this tract of land will be very valuable."[68]

Jennings's sad end came during the sweltering July of 1834. He was fifty years old. Although the cause of death was never publicly stated, heavy drinking likely stood as the main cause of his demise. Tipton lamented to Lanier, "I have received your letter of the 4th of this month announcing the death of my friend Govr Jenings. I lament his death. he has been usefull to me and to my Country, a man of more untarnished Honour never lived—and but for his inordinate thirst for liquor he might have lived and been a most usefull Citizen many years."[69]

Death did not bring peace. Jennings's finances were in disarray, leaving Clarissa Jennings destitute and his creditors, many of them local neighbors, embittered. Tipton, who owned the deed to Jennings's property, wished to cut his losses, but still had great concern for Jennings's widow. In the end, Tipton bailed out, selling the farm to Joseph Carr and giving Jennings's widow "$100 as a present." Tipton wrote Lanier about the transaction: "I am aware that something could have been had for the land but this brings the matter a short close and by it I will not loose more than $150 of which I give mr. Jennings $50."[70]

An immediate result of Jennings's legacy of debt and the resulting bitterness of his creditors was a lack of a marker at the former governor's grave. Indeed, the burial site would have likely been forgotten if a group of schoolchildren had not witnessed the burial and could later tell others where Jennings's body rested. Early in 1861 a bill was introduced in the Indiana General Assembly to erect a monument over Jennings's unmarked grave; the bill failed, as did two other attempts, in 1869 and in 1889. Three years later, the legislature finally agreed to build a seven-and-a-half-foot granite monument in Jennings's honor. About the same time his grave was moved from the abandoned cemetery to a more appropriate site. Three individuals who had witnessed Jennings's burial as children were asked independently of each other to locate the former governor's grave—each one chose the same spot. One of the three, James M. Van Hook, wrote the following account of the opening of the grave: "When the grave was opened there was found some fragments of a cherry coffin. . . . Some people were very skeptical, but I have never had the least doubt as to the earth that was moved to the new cemetery being the true remains of Indiana's famous governor."[71]

As mentioned earlier in this work, historians' assessments of Jennings run a broad spectrum, ranging from overidealized to severely critical. Perhaps Andrew R. L. Cayton's recent observations stand as the most balanced. Cayton believed that while Jennings's political skills and vision primarily involved keeping him "and his allies . . . in power," Jennings served as both governor and representative at a pivotal time when political power in Indiana was changing from a small to a much larger body of citizens. "The shifts from government by patronage to government by election and from the governor to the legislature as the center of political power were not inconsiderable," Cayton has noted. "They reflected a revolution in the style and procedures of politics. To some extent, at least, would-be officeholders had to appeal to their neighbors to secure offices; officially, the source of their authority was not the president of the United States or the Northwest Ordinance or the governor of the Indiana Territory but the narrowly defined conception of 'the people.'" Jennings, Cayton ultimately assessed, "ritually affirmed the end of one political era and the beginning of a new one for the peoples who inhabited the banks of the Wabash River and its many tributaries."[72]

Tellingly, even Jennings's official portraits at the Indiana statehouse convey the same sense of struggle historians have faced in making peace with the state's first governor. The only authentic portrait of this supremely effective politician, painted by Scottish portrait painter James Frobes in 1869, comes from a miniature that Jennings gave to his first wife about 1810. It portrays a young, rather gaunt, and disturbed-looking man with thick, tightly pressed lips. The result of Frobes's interpretation, however, offers a somewhat dapper, more intense-looking man, and not the already world-weary face peering from the miniature. In 1916 Hoosier artist T. C. Steele was commissioned to paint another portrait. Steele's work hardly varied from Frobes's, and both now hang in the statehouse as authentic portrayals of what Jennings looked like. Similar to the either overly idealized or the overly critical historical assessments of Jennings, these portraits seemed to have failed to capture the real person.

Jennings died under circumstances that marked him, in the culture in which he lived, as a failure. Yet Jennings's story contains elements of triumph as well as tragedy. Jennings suffered with alcoholism at a time when American culture had the least understanding of this powerful disease. Jennings's accomplishments, while spotty, still represent an amazing example of perseverance in the face of difficult odds. His stewardship of a state in transition to a more democratic form of government stands as commendable. In this regard, William Woollen's observation seems right: "Indiana owes him more than she can compute."[73]

Introduction

1. John D. Barnhart and Donald F. Carmony, *Indiana: From Frontier to Industrial Commonwealth* (New York: Lewis Historical Publishing Company, 1954), 1:183.

2. Dorothy L. Riker, "Jonathan Jennings," *Indiana Magazine of History* 28 (December 1932): 223.

3. William Woollen, *Biographical and Historical Sketches of Early Indiana* (Indianapolis: Hammond and Company, 1883), 41.

4. Logan Esarey, ed., *Messages and Papers of Jonathan Jennings, Ratliff Boon, William Hendricks, 1816–1825* (Indianapolis: Indiana Historical Commission, 1924), 3:28.

5. Jacob P. Dunn Jr., *Indiana: A Redemption from Slavery* (Boston: Houghton Mifflin, 1905), 389.

6. Woollen, *Biographical and Historical Sketches*, 41.

7. John H. B. Nowland, *Sketches of Prominent Citizens of 1876: With a Few of the Pioneers of the City and County Who Have Passed Away* (Indianapolis: Tilford and Carlon, 1877), 59; and Samuel Ralston, "Jonathan Jennings, First Governor of Indiana," *Proceedings of the Third Annual Conference on Indiana History*, Bulletin No. 15, (February 1922): 53.

8. Oliver H. Smith, *Early Indiana Trials and Sketches: Reminiscences* (Cincinnati: Moore, Wilstach, Keys and Company, 1858), 86.

9. William M. Cockrum, *Pioneer History of Indiana, Including Stories, Incidents, and Customs of the Early Settlers* (Oakland City, IN: Press of Oakland City Journal, 1907), 479.

10. Esarey, ed., *Messages and Papers of Jonathan Jennings, Ratliff Boon, William Hendricks*, 3:28.

11. Logan Esarey, ed., *Messages and Letters of William Henry Harrison*, 2 vols. (Indianapolis: Indiana Historical Commission, 1922), 1:312n2.

12. Riker, "Jonathan Jennings," 239.

13. Barnhart and Carmony, *Indiana*, 1:153.

14. Andrew R. L. Cayton, *Frontier Indiana* (Bloomington: Indiana University Press, 1996), 226.

15. Brent Smith, "The Biography of Jonathan Jennings: Indiana's First Governor" (PhD diss., Ball State University, 1987), 316.

16. Esarey, ed., *Messages and Papers of Jonathan Jennings*, 3:28.

17. Woollen, *Biographical and Historical Sketches*, 39–40.

18. Nellie Armstrong Robertson and Dorothy L. Riker, eds., *The John Tipton Papers*, 3 vols. (Indianapolis: Indiana Historical Bureau, 1942), 3:72.

19. The American Medical Association has defined alcoholism as a disease since 1956.

20. W. J. Rorabaugh, *The Alcoholic Republic: An American Tradition* (New York: Oxford University Press, 1979), 149.

21. In Shirley S. McCord, comp., *Travel Accounts of Indiana, 1679–1961: A Collection of Observations by Wayfaring Foreigners, Itinerants, and Peripatetic Hoosiers* (Indianapolis: Indiana Historical Bureau, 1970), 134.

22. William Warren Sweet, *Revivalism in America: Its Origin, Growth, and Decline* (Gloucester, MA: Peter Smith, 1965), 118.

23. Esarey, ed., *Messages and Letters of William Henry Harrison*, 1:28.

24. Ibid., 1:31.

25. Ibid., 1:35.

26. *Evansville Gazette*, March 24, 1824.

27. Robertson and Riker, eds., *The John Tipton Papers*, 2:618.

28. Dorothy L. Riker, comp., *Unedited Letters of Jonathan Jennings* (Indianapolis: Indiana Historical Society, 1932), 209.

29. Gayle Thornbrough, ed., *The Diary of Calvin Fletcher*, 9 vols. (Indianapolis: Indiana Historical Society, 1972–83), 1:89.

30. Alexis de Tocqueville, *Democracy in America*, 2 vols. (New York: Alfred A. Knopf, 1963), 1:31.

31. Frances Trollope, *Domestic Manners of the Americans* (New York: Alfred A. Knopf, 1949), 255.

32. Tocqueville, *Democracy in America*, 396.

33. *Evansville Gazette*, March 24, 1824.

34. *Evansville Gazette*, June 11, 1823.

35. Robertson and Riker, eds., *The John Tipton Papers*, 3:667.

Chapter 1

1. Dorothy L. Riker, comp., *Unedited Letters of Jonathan Jennings* (Indianapolis: Indiana Historical Society, 1932), 158.

2. *Vincennes Western Sun*, November 4, 1826.

3. For a detailed genealogy of the Jennings clan see Eileen Stockman Jennings, *The Jennings Family: Descendants of David Jennings* (Marceline, MO: Walsworth Publishing Company, 1976).

4. A Jennings family tree can be found in Riker, comp., *Unedited Letters of Jonathan Jennings*, 152.

5. Riker, comp., *Unedited Letters of Jonathan Jennings*, 165.

6. Adade Mitchell Wheeler and Marlene Stein Wortman, *The Roads They Made: Women in Illinois History* (Chicago: Charles H. Kerr Publishing Co., 1977), 28.

7. Riker, comp., *Unedited Letters of Jonathan Jennings*, 219.

8. Ibid., 157–58.

9. Ibid., 158.

10. Ibid.

11. Ibid., 159.

12. Ibid.

13. Ibid., 199.

14. Ibid., 264.

15. Brent Smith, "The Biography of Jonathan Jennings: Indiana's First Governor" (PhD diss., Ball State University, 1987), 315.

16. William Faux, *Memorable Days in America: Being a Journal of a Tour to the United States*, in Reuben Gold Thwaites, *Early Western Travels*, 2 vols. (Cleveland: Arthur H. Clark Co., 1905), 1:285.

17. Riker, comp., *Unedited Letters of Jonathan Jennings*, 160.

18. Ibid., 262.

19. Otto L. Schmidt, "The Mississippi Valley in 1816 through an Englishman's Diary," *Mississippi Valley Historical Review* 14 (September 1927): 146.

20. Riker, comp., *Unedited Letters of Jonathan Jennings*, 160–161.

Chapter 2

1. Reuben Gold Thwaites, ed., *Early Western Travels; 1748–1846*, vol. 10 (Cleveland, OH: Arthur H. Clark Company, 1904), 10:247.

2. James Hall, *Letters from the West: Containing Sketches of Scenery, Manners, and Customs; and Anecdotes Connected with the First Settlements of the Western Sections of the United States* (1828; reprint, Gainesville, FL: Scholars' Facsimiles and Reprints, 1967), 139.

3. Harlow Lindley, ed., *Indiana as Seen by Early Travelers: A Collection of Reprints from Books of Travel, Letters and Diaries Prior to 1830* (Indianapolis: Indiana Historical Bureau, 1916), 19.

4. Ibid., 21.

5. Ibid., 21–22.

6. Ibid., 22.

7. Logan Esarey, ed., *Messages and Letters of William Henry Harrison*, 2 vols. (Indianapolis: Indiana Historical Commission, 1922), 1:28.

8. Lindley, ed., *Indiana as Seen by Early Travelers*, 23.

9. Esarey, ed., *Messages and Letters of William Henry Harrison*, 1:261.

10. Lindley, ed., *Indiana as Seen by Early Travelers*, 101.

11. Shirley S. McCord, ed., *Travel Accounts of Indiana, 1679–1961: A Collection of Observations by Wayfaring Foreigners, Itinerants, and Peripatetic Hoosiers* (Indianapolis: Indiana Historical Bureau, 1970), 117.

12. Lindley, ed., *Indiana as Seen by Early Travelers*, 252.

13. Ibid., 246–47.

14. Ibid., 301.

15. Adlard Welby, *A Visit to North America and the English Settlements in Illinois, with a Winter Residence at Philadelphia*, in

Reuben Gold Thwaites, ed., *Early Western Travels*, 2 vols. (Cleveland: Arthur H. Clark, 1905), 2:229.

16. Gayle Thornbrough, ed., *The Correspondence of John Badollet and Albert Gallatin, 1804–1836* (Indianapolis: Indiana Historical Society, 1963), 94.

17. Morris Birkbeck, *Notes on a Journey in America: From the Coast of Virginia to the Territory of Illinois* (London: Severns and Company, 1818), 87.

18. Thwaites, ed., *Early Western Travels*, 1:292.

19. Lindley, ed., *Indiana As Seen by Early Travelers*, 306.

20. Elliott J. Gorn, "Gauge and Bite, Pull Hair and Scratch: The Social Significance of Fighting in Southern Back Country," *American Historical Review* 90 (February 1985): 26.

21. Thwaites, ed., *Early Western Travels*, 10:255; Thomas Twining, *Travels in America 100 Years Ago* (New York: Harper and Brothers, 1894), 89–90.

22. Gayle Thornbrough and Dorothy L. Riker, comps., *Readings in Indiana History* (Indianapolis: Indiana Historical Bureau, 1956), 482.

23. Frances Trollope, *Domestic Manners of the Americans*, Donald Smalley, ed. (New York: Alfred A. Knopf, 1949), 179.

24. Esarey, ed., *Messages and Letters of William Henry Harrison*, 1:34.

25. Mary M. Crawford, ed., "Mrs. Lydia B. Bacon's Journal, 1811–1812," *Indiana Magazine of History* 40 (December 1944): 380.

26. Lindley, ed., *Indiana as Seen by Early Travelers*, 315.

27. Dorothy L. Riker, comp., *Unedited Letters of Jonathan Jennings* (Indianapolis: Indiana Historical Society, 1932), 165–66.

28. Gayle Thornbrough, ed., *The Correspondence of John Badollet and Albert Gallatin, 1804–1836* (Indianapolis: Indiana Historical Society, 1963), 37.

29. In Gladys Scott Thomson, *A Pioneer Family: The Birkbecks in Illinois, 1818–1827* (London: Jonathan Cape, 1953), 116.

30. Lindley, ed., *Indiana as Seen by Early Travelers*, 320.

31. *Vincennes Western Sun*, September 3, 1808.

32. William Woollen, *Biographical and Historical Sketches of Early Indiana* (Indianapolis: Hammond and Company, 1883) 41.

33. Riker, comp., *Unedited Letters of Jonathan Jennings*, 163.

34. Ibid.

35. John A. Jakle, *Images of the Ohio Valley: A Historical Geography of Travel, 1740 to 1860* (New York: Oxford University Press, 1977), 45.

36. Jonathan Jennings to David Mitchell, September 19, 1807, William H. English Collection, Special Collections Research Center, University of Chicago Library.

37. Riker, comp., *Unedited Letters of Jonathan Jennings*, 164.

38. McCord, ed., *Travel Accounts of Indiana*, 134.

39. Crawford, "Mrs. Lydia B. Bacon's Journal," 380.

40. Thornbrough, ed., *Correspondence of John Badollet and Albert Gallatin*, 20–21.

41. Ibid., 58.

42. Riker, comp., *Unedited Letters of Jonathan Jennings*, 161.

Chapter 3

1. Dorothy B. Goebel, *William Henry Harrison: A Political Biography* (Indianapolis: Historical Bureau of the Indiana Library and Historical Department, 1926), 51.

2. John D. Barnhart, ed., "Letters of William H. Harrison to Thomas Worthington, 1799–1813," *Indiana Magazine of History* 47 (March 1951): 58.

3. Ibid., 60.

4. Goebel, *William Henry Harrison*, 57.

5. Ibid.

6. Logan Esarey, ed., *Messages and Letters of William Henry Harrison*, 2 vols. (Indianapolis: Indiana Historical Commission, 1922), 1:34–35.

7. Barnhart, ed., "Letters of William H. Harrison to Thomas Worthington," 62, and Esarey, ed., *Messages and Letters of William Henry Harrison*, 1:34.

8. Esarey, ed., *Messages and Letters of William Henry Harrison*, 1:108.

9. Ibid., 1:35.

10. Ibid.

11. Ibid., 1:1.

12. Ibid., 1:127.

13. Ibid., 1:87.

14. Ibid., 1:517.

15. John D. Barnhart, ed., "The Letters of Decius," *Indiana Magazine of History* 43 (September 1947): 271.

16. Esarey, ed., *Messages and Letters of William Henry Harrison*, 1:297.

17. Ibid.

18. Andrew R. L. Cayton, *Frontier Indiana* (Bloomington: Indiana University Press, 1996), 233.

19. Esarey, ed., *Messages and Letters of William Henry Harrison*, 1:196.

20. William Woollen, *Biographical and Historical Sketches of Early Indiana* (Indianapolis: Hammond and Company, 1883), 391–92.

21. *Vincennes Western Sun*, August 27, 1804.

22. Barnhart, "The Letters of Decius," 272–76.

23. Ibid., 274.

24. Ibid., 292.

25. Ibid., 281.

26. Ibid., 274.

27. Earl E. McDonald, "Disposal of Negro Slaves by Will in Knox County, Indiana," *Indiana Magazine of History* 26 (June 1930): 143–46.

28. Ibid., 144.

29. Ibid., 145.

30. *History of Gibson County, Indiana, with Illustrations Descriptive of Its Scenery, and Biographical Sketches of Some of Its Prominent Men and Pioneers* (Edwardsville, IL: Jas. T. Tartt and Company, 1884), 78.

31. Emma Lou Thornbrough, *The Negro in Indiana: A Study of a Minority* (Indianapolis: Indiana Historical Bureau, 1957), 10.

32. Gayle Thornbrough, ed., *The Correspondence of John Badollet and Albert Gallatin, 1804–1836* (Indianapolis: Indiana Historical Society, 1963), 97.

33. Emma Lou Thornbrough, *The Negro in Indiana*, 11.

34. Ibid., 12.

35. Barnhart, ed., "Letters of William H. Harrison to Thomas Worthington," 67.

36. Esarey, ed., *Messages and Letters of William Henry Harrison*, 1:265.

37. Thornbrough, ed., *Correspondence of John Badollet and Albert Gallatin*, 17–18.

38. Ibid., 18.

39. Ibid., 42.

40. Ibid., 30.

41. Ibid., 44.

42. Ibid., 46.

43. Ibid., 48.

44. Ibid., 61–62.

45. Ibid., 63.

46. Ibid., 65.

47. Ibid., 73–74.

48. Ibid., 101.

49. Ibid., 101–02.

50. Ibid., 107, 111.

51. Ibid., 112.

52. Ibid., 40.

53. Ibid., 49.

54. Ibid., 64.

55. Ibid., 65.

56. Ibid., 91, 93.

57. Ibid., 97.

58. Ibid., 102.

59. Ibid., 104–05.

60. Barnhart, ed., "Letters of William H. Harrison to Thomas Worthington," 73.

Chapter 4

1. Gayle Thornbrough, ed., *The Correspondence of John Badollet and Albert Gallatin, 1804–1836* (Indianapolis: Indiana Historical Society, 1963), 68.

2. Ibid., 69–70.

3. Ibid., 98.

4. Ibid., 44.

5. Ibid., 116.

6. See Richard Power, *Planting Corn Belt Culture: The Impress of the Upland Southerner and Yankee in the Old Northwest* (Indianapolis: Indiana Historical Society, 1953); and Nicole Etcheson, *The Emerging Midwest: Upland Southerners and the Political Culture of the Old Northwest, 1787–1861* (Bloomington: Indiana University Press, 1996).

7. John S. Wright, *Letters From the West, or a Caution to Emigrants: Being Facts and Observations Respecting the States of Ohio, Indiana, Illinois, and Some Parts of New York, Pennsylvania, and Kentucky* (Salem, NY: Dodd and Stevenson, 1819), 21, 24.

8. Thornbrough, ed., *Correspondence of John Badollet and Albert Gallatin*, 58.

9. James H. Madison, *The Indiana Way: A State History* (Bloomington: Indiana University Press; Indianapolis: Indiana Historical Society, 1986), 62.

10. Peirce Lewis, "American Roots in Pennsylvania Soil," in E. Willard Miller, ed., *A Geography of Pennsylvania* (University Park: Pennsylvania State University Press, 1995).

11. Thornbrough, ed., *Correspondence of John Badollet and Albert Gallatin*, 65.

12. Ibid., 204.

13. William Faux, *Memorable Days in America: Being a Journal of a Tour to the United States*, in Ruben Gold Thwaites, ed., *Early Western Travels*, 2 vols. (Cleveland, OH: Arthur H. Clark Co., 1905), 1:282.

14. Mary M. Crawford, ed., "Mrs. Lydia B. Bacon's Journal, 1811–1812," *Indiana Magazine of History* 40 (December 1944): 381.

15. Thomas Twining, *Travels in America 100 Years Ago* (New York: Harper and Brothers, 1894), 90–91.

16. Thornbrough, ed., *Correspondence of John Badollet and Albert Gallatin*, 98.

17. Dorothy L. Riker, comp., *Unedited Letters of Jonathan Jennings* (Indianapolis: Indiana Historical Society, 1932), 161.

18. Ibid., 164.

19. Ibid., 161–62.

20. Ibid., 162.

21. Ibid., 94.

22. Ibid., 102–03.

23. Lee Burns, *Life in Old Vincennes* (Indianapolis: Indiana Historical Society, 1929), 455.

24. Riker, comp., *Unedited Letters of Jonathan Jennings*, 162–163.

25. Thornbrough, ed., *Correspondence of John Badollet and Albert Gallatin*, 78.

26. Ibid., 96.

27. Ibid., 82.

28. Ibid., 81.

29. Ibid., 106–07.

30. Riker, comp., *Unedited Letters of Jonathan Jennings*, 163.

31. Gayle Thornbrough and Dorothy L. Riker, eds., *Journals of the General Assembly of Indiana Territory, 1805–1815* (Indianapolis: Indiana Historical Bureau, 1950), 974.

32. Robert Constantine, ed., "Minutes of the Board of Trustees for Vincennes University," *Indiana Magazine of History* 54 (December 1958): 313–65.

33. Thornbrough and Riker, eds., *Journals of the General Assembly of Indiana Territory*, 987.

34. Constantine, "Minutes of the Board of Trustees for Vincennes University," 358.

35. Ibid.

36. *Vincennes Western Sun*, August 20, 1808.

37. Robert Constantine, ed., "Minutes of the Board of Trustees for Vincennes University (October 16, 1807–December 11, 1811)" *Indiana Magazine of History* 55 (September 1959), 258, 263.

38. *Vincennes Western Sun*, April 20, 1808.

39. Thornbrough, ed., *Correspondence of John Badollet and Albert Gallatin*, 177–78.

40. Ibid., 107.

41. Riker, comp., *Unedited Letters of Jonathan Jennings*, 162.

42. Ibid., 164.

43. Thornbrough, ed., *Correspondence of John Badollet and Albert Gallatin*, 103.

Chapter 5

1. Dorothy L. Riker, comp., *Unedited Letters of Jonathan Jennings* (Indianapolis: Indiana Historical Society, 1932), 165.

2. Ibid., 166–67.

3. Ibid., 166.

4. Ibid.

5. Ibid., 167–68.

6. "Some Additional Jennings Letters," *Indiana Magazine of History* 39 (September 1943): 280–81.

7. Ibid.

8. *Vincennes Western Sun*, January 28, 1809; February 4, 1809; and February 11, 1809.

9. *Vincennes Western Sun*, February 23, 1809.

10. Jacob P. Dunn Jr., *Indiana: A Redemption from Slavery* (Boston: Houghton Mifflin, 1905), 390.

11. Ibid., 393.

12. Riker, comp., *Unedited Letters of Jonathan Jennings*, 171.

13. Dunn, *Indiana*, 395.

14. Ibid., 395–96.

15. Ibid., 396.

16. *Vincennes Western Sun*, March 11, 1809; April 27, 1809; and April 29, 1809.

17. Gayle Thornbrough, ed., *The Correspondence of John Badollet and Albert Gallatin, 1804–1836* (Indianapolis: Indiana Historical Society, 1963), 124.

18. Dunn, *Indiana*, 398.

19. William Woollen, *Biographical and Historical Sketches of Early Indiana* (Indianapolis: Hammond and Company, 1883), 397.

20. Thornbrough, ed., *Correspondence of John Badollet and Albert Gallatin*, 127, 129.

21. Ibid., 114.

22. Ibid., 110.

23. Woollen, *Biographical and Historical Sketches*, 394–95.

24. *Vincennes Western Sun*, July 8, 1809.

25. Thornbrough, ed., *Correspondence of John Badollet and Albert Gallatin*, 130.

26. Riker, comp., *Unedited Letters of Jonathan Jennings*, 169.

27. "Some Additional Jennings Letters," 281.

28. Riker, comp., *Unedited Letters of Jonathan Jennings*, 173–74.

29. Woollen, *Biographical and Historical Sketches*, 393.

30. Ibid.

31. Riker, comp., *Unedited Letters of Jonathan Jennings*, 172–74.

32. Ibid.

33. Woollen, *Biographical and Historical Sketches*, 393.

34. Ibid., 32.

35. Thornbrough, ed., *Correspondence of John Badollet and Albert Gallatin*, 119.

36. Ibid.

37. Ibid., 120.

38. Woollen, *Biographical and Historical Sketches*, 395–96.

Chapter 6

1. Lonnelle Aikman, *We, the People: The Story of the United States Capitol: Its Past and Its Promise* (Washington, DC: United States Capitol Historical Society, 1963), 25.

2. Saul K. Padover, ed., *Thomas Jefferson and the National Capital* (Washington, DC: United States Government Printing Office, 1946), 386.

3. Ibid., 446–47.

4. Mary Cable, *The Avenue of the Presidents* (Boston: Houghton Mifflin, 1969), 16.

5. William Henry Harrison letter to W. E. Nicholson, November 21, 1809, William Henry Harrison Papers, William Henry Smith Memorial Library, Indiana Historical Society, Indianapolis.

6. Dorothy L. Riker, comp., *Unedited Letters of Jonathan Jennings* (Indianapolis: Indiana Historical Society, 1932), 172, 174–75.

7. Ibid., 175–76.

8. "Some Additional Jennings Letters," *Indiana Magazine of History* 39 (September 1943): 281–82.

9. Riker, comp., *Unedited Letters of Jonathan Jennings*, 176.

10. Ibid., 175.

11. "Some Additional Jennings Letters," 281–82.

12. Riker, comp., *Unedited Letters of Jonathan Jennings*, 177.

13. *Annals of Congress*, 11th Congr., 3rd sess., 1659–60.

14. Gayle Thornbrough, ed., *The Correspondence of John Badollet and Albert Gallatin, 1804–1836* (Indianapolis: Indiana Historical Society, 1963), 166.

15. Ibid., 127–28.

16. Ibid., 166.

17. Ibid., 175, 181.

18. Logan Esarey, ed., *Messages and Letters of William Henry Harrison*, 2 vols. (Indianapolis: Indiana Historical Commission, 1922), 1:502–03.

19. Ibid., 1:501–502.

20. Thornbrough, ed., *Correspondence of John Badollet and Albert Gallatin*, 191.

21. *Vincennes Western Sun*, December 15, 1810.

22. Thornbrough, ed., *Correspondence of John Badollet and Albert Gallatin*, 191–92.

23. Brent Smith, "The Biography of Jonathan Jennings: Indiana's First Governor" (PhD dissertation, Ball State University, 1987), 99.

24. Ibid., 100.

25. Riker, comp., *Unedited Letters of Jonathan Jennings*, 178.

26. Ibid.

27. Mabel C. Morrison, *Ann Gilmore Hay: Wife of Jonathan Jennings from 1811 to 1826* (Indianapolis: John E. Hampton, 1925), 12.

28. Ibid.

29. Riker, comp., *Unedited Letters of Jonathan Jennings*, 178.

30. Ibid., 180–81.

31. Ibid., 181–82.

32. Ibid., 182.

33. Morrison, *Ann Gilmore Hay*, 14.

34. Riker, comp., *Unedited Letters of Jonathan Jennings*, 188.

35. Ibid.

36. Ibid., 191–92.

37. "Some Additional Jennings Letters," 283.

38. Ibid.

39. Ibid., 284.

40. Ibid., 286.

41. Ibid., 287.

42. Ibid., 288.

43. Ibid.

44. Riker, comp., *Unedited Letters of Jonathan Jennings*, 192.

45. Thornbrough, ed., *Correspondence of John Badollet and Albert Gallatin*, 253.

46. Riker, comp., *Unedited Letters of Jonathan Jennings*, 194.

47. Ibid., 195.

48. Thornbrough, ed., *Correspondence of John Badollet and Albert Gallatin*, 169–71.

49. "Some Additional Jennings Letters," 282.

50. Thornbrough, ed., *Correspondence of John Badollet and Albert Gallatin*, 206, 226.

51. Ibid., 206.

52. Ibid., 220.

53. Mary M. Crawford, ed., "Mrs. Lydia B. Bacon's Journal, 1811–1812," *Indiana Magazine of History* 40 (December 1944): 384.

54. In William Woollen, *Biographical and Historical Sketches of Early Indiana* (Indianapolis: Hammond and Company, 1883), 398–99.

55. Robert S. Lambert, "The Conduct of the Militia at Tippecanoe: Elihu Stout's Controversy with Colonel John P. Boyd, January, 1812," *Indiana Magazine of History* 51 (September 1955): 238.

56. Ibid., 240.

57. Thornbrough, ed., *Correspondence of John Badollet and Albert Gallatin*, 208.

58. John D. Barnhart, ed., "Letters of William H. Harrison to Thomas Worthington, 1799–1813," *Indiana Magazine of History* 47 (March 1951): 73.

59. *Vincennes Western Sun*, June 2, 1812.

60. Riker, ed., *Correspondence of John Badollet and Albert Gallatin*, 243.

61. Esarey, ed., *Messages and Letters of William H. Harrison*, 2:29–30.

62. Riker, comp., *Unedited Letters of Jonathan Jennings*, 189.

63. "Some Additional Jennings Letters," 283.

64. Riker, comp., *Unedited Letters of Jonathan Jennings*, 201.

65. Ibid., 181.

66. Thornbrough, ed., *Correspondence of John Badollet and Albert Gallatin*, 244.

67. *Vincennes Western Sun*, June 23, 1812.

68. Logan Esarey, ed., *Messages and Papers of Jonathan Jennings, Ratliff Boon, William Hendricks* (Indianapolis: Indiana Historical Commission, 1924), 3:29.

69. Ibid., 3:29–32.

70. *Vincennes Western Sun*, July 11, 1823, and July 23, 1823.

71. Riker, comp., *Unedited Letters of Jonathan Jennings*, 189.

72. "Some Additional Jennings Letters," 289.

73. Riker, comp., *Unedited Letters of Jonathan Jennings*, 199.

74. Esarey, ed., *Messages and Papers of Jonathan Jennings, Ratliff Boon, William Hendricks*, 3:29.

75. Riker, comp., *Unedited Letters of Jonathan Jennings*, 203.

76. Ibid., 209–10.

77. "Some Additional Jennings Letters," 290.

Chapter 7

1. John D. Barnhart and Donald F. Carmony, *Indiana: From Frontier to Industrial Commonwealth*, 4 vols. (New York: Lewis Historical Publishing Company, 1954), 1:143.

2. Gayle Thornbrough, ed., *The Correspondence of John Badollet and Albert Gallatin, 1804–1836* (Indianapolis: Indiana Historical Society, 1963), 212.

3. Barnhart and Carmony, *Indiana*, 1:150.

4. Jacob P. Dunn Jr., *Indiana: A Redemption from Slavery* (Boston: Houghton Mifflin, 1905), 418.

5. *Vincennes Western Sun*, April 20, 1816.

6. Ibid.

7. "Some Additional Jennings Letters," *Indiana Magazine of History* 39 (September 1943): 290.

8. *Vincennes Western Sun*, April 20, 1816.

9. *Vincennes Western Sun*, May 2, 1816.

10. Barnhart and Carmony, *Indiana*, 1:150.

11. Ibid., 1:150–151.

12. Ibid., 1:153.

13. Justin E. Walsh, *The Centennial History of the Indiana General Assembly, 1816–1978* (Indianapolis: The Select Committee on the Centennial History of the Indiana General Assembly, 1987), 45.

14. Thornbrough, ed., *Correspondence of John Badollet and Albert Gallatin*, 261–262.

15. "Some Additional Jennings Letters," 290–91.

16. John B. Dillon, *A History of Indiana* (Indianapolis: Bingham and Doughty, 1859), 559.

17. Dunn, *Indiana*, 389, and Barnhart and Carmony, *Indiana*, 1:153.

18. Andrew R. L. Cayton, *Frontier Indiana* (Bloomington: Indiana University Press, 1996), 226–27.

19. Barnhart and Carmony, *Indiana*, 1:151.

20. "Journal of the Convention of the Indiana Territory," *Indiana Magazine of History* 61 (June 1965): 77–155.

21. Ibid., 94.

22. Ibid.

23. Dunn, *Indiana*, 441. See also Walsh, *Centennial History of the Indiana General Assembly*, chapter five, for detailed information regarding the treatment of blacks by the general assembly in early Indiana history.

24. "To his Excellency Thomas Posey," petition from Harrison County, Indiana, March 10, 1814, William H. English Collection, Special Collections Center, University of Chicago.

25. *Vincennes Western Sun*, July 6, 1816, and July 27, 1816.

26. *Vincennes Western Sun*, September 7, 1816.

27. Samuel Merrill, in Charles Moores, "Old Corydon," *Indiana Magazine of History* 13 (March 1917): 24.

28. William Woollen, *Biographical and Historical Sketches of Early Indiana* (Indianapolis: Hammond and Company, 1883), 26.

29. Riker, comp., *Unedited Letters of Jonathan Jennings*, 220.

30. Ibid., 223–24.

31. Mabel C. Morrison, *Ann Gilmore Hay: Wife of Jonathan Jennings from 1811 to 1826* (Indianapolis: John E. Hampton, 1925), 23.

32. Riker, comp., *Unedited Letters of Jonathan Jennings*, 223, 218–19.

33. Ibid., 218.

34. Morrison, *Ann Gilmore Hay*, 21–2.

35. Adam A. Leonard, "Personal Politics in Indiana 1816 to 1840," *Indiana Magazine of History* 19 (March 1923): 1.

36. Barnhart and Carmony, *Indiana*, 1:181.

37. *Evansville Gazette*, July 13, 1822.

38. *Evansville Gazette*, July 6, 1822.

39. Gayle Thornbrough, ed., *The Diary of Calvin Fletcher*, 9 vols. (Indianapolis: Indianapolis Historical Society, 1972), 1:87.

40. Nellie Armstrong Robertson and Dorothy Riker, eds., *The John Tipton Papers*, 3 vols. (Indianapolis: Indiana Historical Bureau, 1942), 2:626.

41. Ibid., 2:677.

42. Walsh, *Centennial History of the Indiana General Assembly*, 79.

43. Thornbrough, ed., *Diary of Calvin Fletcher*, 1:99.

44. *Evansville Gazette*, June 1, 1824.

45. Robertson and Riker, *The John Tipton Papers*, 2:695.

46. *Evansville Gazette*, July 8, 1824.

47. *Indiana Centennial*, March 17, 1821.

48. *Evansville Gazette*, May 28, 1825, and June 4, 1825.

49. Riker, comp., *Unedited Letters of Jonathan Jennings*, 214.

50. Karl Arndt, ed., *A Documentary History of the Indiana Decade of the Harmony Society 1814–1824*, 2 vols. (Indianapolis: Indiana Historical Society, 1975), 1:215.

51. Riker, comp., *Unedited Letters of Jonathan Jennings*, 223.

52. Karl Arndt, *George Rapp's Harmony Society 1785–1847* (Philadelphia: University of Pennsylvania Press, 1965), 263.

53. Arndt, ed., *Documentary History*, 1:358.

54. Ibid., 1:742.

55. Ibid., 1:659.

56. Ibid., 1:670–71.

57. Ibid., 2:124.

58. Ibid., 2:298.

59. *Corydon Gazette*, November 8, 1821.

60. Arndt, ed., *Documentary History*, 2:439–40.

61. Ibid., 2:449–50.

62. Woollen, *Biographical and Historical Sketches*, 162.

63. Ibid., 163.

64. Logan Esarey, ed., *Messages and Papers of Jonathan Jennings, Ratliff Boon, William Hendricks, 1816–1825* (Indianapolis: Indiana Historical Commission, 1924), 3:56–57.

65. Donald Carmony, *Indiana, 1816–1850: The Pioneer Era* (Indianapolis: Indiana Historical Bureau and Indiana Historical Society, 1998), 26.

66. *Vincennes Western Sun*, November 14, 1818.

67. Jacob P. Dunn Jr., *Indiana and Indianans: A History of Aboriginal and Territorial Indiana and the Century of Statehood*, 5 vols. (Chicago: American Historical Society, 1919), 1:375–77.

68. *Madison Western Clarion*, July 24, 1822.

69. *Jeffersonville Indianian*, July 3, 1818.

70. *Vincennes Western Sun*, October 3, 1818.

71. *Indiana Senate Journal*, 1818–19, pp. 5–7.

72. Esarey, ed., *Messages and Papers of Jonathan Jennings, Ratliff Boon, William Hendricks*, 3:69.

73. *Indiana House Journal*, 1818–19, pp. 41–42, 55–56.

74. Esarey, ed., *Messages and Papers of Jonathan Jennings, Ratliff Boon, William Hendricks*, 3:62.

75. "Some Additional Jennings Letters," 292.

76. Robertson and Riker, eds., *The John Tipton Papers*, 2:156.

77. Ibid., 2:157.

78. *Vincennes Western Sun*, July 31, 1819.

79. *Vincennes Western Sun*, July 24, 1819.

80. Ibid.

81. *Vincennes Western Sun*, July 21, 1821.

82. Carmony, *Indiana, 1816–1850*, 29.

83. Cayton, *Frontier Indiana*, 259.

84. Thornbrough, ed., *Diary of Calvin Fletcher*, 2:168.

85. Nicole Etcheson, *The Emerging Midwest: Upland Southerners and the Political Culture of the Old Northwest, 1787–1861* (Bloomington: Indiana University Press, 1996).

86. Esarey, ed., *Messages and Letters of Jonathan Jennings, Ratliff Boon, William Hendricks*, 3:42.

87. Arthur Blythe, "A Biographical Sketch of Jonathan Jennings" (master's thesis, Indiana University, 1921), 135. This work used an earlier copy of Blythe's final master's thesis at Indiana University. The copy can be found at Indiana University's Lilly Library.

88. Riker, comp., *Unedited Letters of Jonathan Jennings*, 218.

Chapter 8

1. Oliver H. Smith, *Early Indiana Trials and Sketches: Reminiscences* (Cincinnati: Moore, Wilstach, Keys and Company, 1858), 84.

2. *Corydon Gazette*, August 8, 1822.

3. *Madison Western Clarion*, July 24, 1822.

4. Dorothy L. Riker, comp., *Unedited Letters of Jonathan Jennings* (Indianapolis: Indiana Historical Society, 1932), 246.

5. Ibid., 235.

6. Ibid., 236.

7. *Madison Western Clarion*, July 24, 1822.

8. Karl Arndt, ed., *A Documentary History of the Indiana Decade of the Harmony Society 1814–1824*, 2 vols. (Indianapolis: Indiana Historical Society, 1978), 2:433.

9. Dorothy L. Riker and Gayle Thornbrough, comps., *Indiana Election Returns, 1816–1851* (Indianapolis: Indiana Historical Bureau, 1960), 75, 77.

10. "Some Additional Jennings Letters," *Indiana Magazine of History* 39 (September 1943): 293.

11. Frances Trollope, *Domestic Manners of the Americans*, ed. Donald Smalley (New York: Alfred A. Knopf, 1949), 227.

12. Ibid., 226.

13. Ibid., 234.

14. Frederick Marryat, *A Diary in America: with Remarks on Its Institutions* (New York: Alfred A. Knopf, 1962), 157.

15. Tipton's journal account of this event can be found in Nellie Armstrong Robertson and Dorothy L. Riker, eds., *The John Tipton Papers*, 3 vols. (Indianapolis: Indiana Historical Bureau, 1942), 1:195–210.

16. Justin Walsh, *The Centennial History of the Indiana General Assembly, 1816-1978* (Indianapolis: The Select Committee on the Centennial History of the Indiana General Assembly, 1987), 121.

17. Riker, comp., *Unedited Letters of Jonathan Jennings*, 255.

18. Robertson and Riker, eds., *The John Tipton Papers*, 2:279.

19. Riker, comp., *Unedited Letters of Jonathan Jennings*, 252–53.

20. Ibid., 252, note 1.

21. "Some Additional Jennings Letters," 295.

22. Riker, comp., *Unedited Letters of Jonathan Jennings*, 219, note 1.

23. Ibid., 251.

24. Ibid., 261–62.

25. Ibid., 264.

26. Robertson and Riker, eds., *The John Tipton Papers*, 1:713.

27. Ibid., 1:690.

28. Ibid., 1:785.

29. Adam A. Leonard, "Personal Politics in Indiana," *Indiana Magazine of History* 19 (March 1923): 29.

30. James F. Hopkins and Mary W. M. Hargreaves, eds., *The Papers of Henry Clay*, 11 vols. (Lexington: University Press of Kentucky, 1973), 5:918.

31. *Vincennes Western Sun*, November 4, 1826.

32. Ibid.

33. Hopkins and Hargreaves, eds., *The Papers of Henry Clay*, 5:918.

34. *Vincennes Western Sun*, November 4, 1826.

35. Hopkins and Hargreaves, eds., *The Papers of Henry Clay*, 5:918–19.

36. Riker, comp., *Unedited Letters of Jonathan Jennings*, 270.

37. Ibid., 270–71.

38. Ibid., 271.

39. "Some Additional Jennings Letters," 293.

40. Riker, comp., *Unedited Letters of Jonathan Jennings*, 270.

41. Robertson and Riker, eds., *The John Tipton Papers*, 2:199.

42. *Vincennes Western Sun*, December 30, 1826.

43. *Indiana Journal*, July 24, 1828.

44. The American Medical Association classified alcoholism as an illness or disease in 1956. As an illness, it is chronic, progressive, incurable, and often includes loss of control. It is, however, treatable through approaches such as twelve-step programs.

45. W. J. Rorabaugh, *The Alcoholic Republic: An American Tradition* (New York: Oxford University Press, 1979), 19, 91.

46. John E. Iglehart, "The Coming of the English to Indiana in 1817 and Their Neighbors," *Indiana Magazine of History* 15 (June 1919): 151.

47. William Warren Sweet, *Revivalism in America: Its Origin, Growth, and Decline* (Glouchester, MA: Peter Smith, 1965), 118.

48. Records of the Posey County, Indiana, Commissioners, 1816, 1817; Warrick County, Indiana Court Records, 1813.

49. Gayle Thornbrough, ed., *The Diary of Calvin Fletcher*, 9 vols. (Indianapolis: Indiana Historical Society, 1972–83), 1:85.

50. R. C. Buley, *The Old Northwest: Pioneer Period, 1815–1840*, 2 vols. (Indianapolis: Indiana Historical Society, 1950), 2:37.

51. Charles Moores, "Old Corydon," *Indiana Magazine of History* 13 (March 1917): 36.

52. Susan Cheever, *My Name is Bill: Bill Wilson: His Life and the Creation of Alcoholics Anonymous* (New York: Simon and Schuster, 2004).

53. Gerald Govorchin, "The Political Life of Jonathan Jennings, First Governor of the State of Indiana" (master's thesis, University of Chicago, 1942), 87.

54. Robertson and Riker, eds., *The John Tipton Papers*, 2:279.

55. Ibid.

56. Riker, comp., *Unedited Letters of Jonathan Jennings*, 273.

57. Joy Julien Bailey, "Notes on Jonathan Jennings," Indiana Division, Indiana State Library, Indianapolis.

58. Robertson and Riker, eds., *The John Tipton Papers*, 2:213.

59. Ibid., 2:666.

60. Ibid., 2:524.

61. Ibid., 2:650.

62. Ibid., 2:666–67.

63. Ibid., 2:752–53, note 46.

64. Ibid., 2:742–743.

65. Ibid., 2:629–30.

66. Ibid., 2:863.

67. Ibid., 3:48.

68. Ibid., 3:64–65.

69. Ibid., 3:72.

70. Ibid., 3:79–80.

71. Bailey, "Notes on Jonathan Jennings."

72. Andrew R. L. Cayton, *Frontier Indiana* (Bloomington, IN: Indiana University Press, 1996), 259–60.

73. William Woollen, *Biographical and Historical Sketches of Early Indiana* (Indianapolis: Hammond and Company, 1883), 41.

SELECT BIBLIOGRAPHY

Arndt, Karl, ed. *A Documentary History of the Indiana Decade of the Harmony Society 1814–1824*. 2 vols. Indianapolis: Indiana Historical Society, 1975–78.

———. *George Rapp's Harmony Society 1785–1847*. Philadelphia: University of Pennsylvania Press, 1965.

Barnhart, John D., and Donald F. Carmony. *Indiana: From Frontier to Industrial Commonwealth*. 4 vols. New York: Lewis Historical Publishing Company, 1954.

Birkbeck, Morris. *Notes on a Journey in America: From the Coast of Virginia to the Territory of Illinois*. London: Severns and Co., 1818.

Blythe, Arthur. "A Biographical Sketch of Jonathan Jennings." Master's thesis, Indiana University, 1921.

Buley, R. Carlyle. *The Old Northwest: Pioneer Period, 1815–1840*. 2 vols. Indianapolis: Indiana Historical Society, 1950.

Burns, Lee. *Life in Old Vincennes*. Indianapolis: Indiana Historical Society, 1929.

Carmony, Donald. *Indiana, 1816–1850: The Pioneer Era*. The History of Indiana, vol. 2. Indianapolis: Indiana Historical Bureau and Indiana Historical Society, 1998.

Cayton, Andrew R. L. *Frontier Indiana*. Bloomington, IN: Indiana University Press, 1996.

Cheever, Susan. *My Name is Bill: His Life and The Creation of Alcoholics Anonymous*. New York: Simon and Schuster, 2004.

Cockrum, William M. *Pioneer History of Indiana, Including Stories, Incidents, and Customs of the Early Settlers*. Oakland City, IN: Press of Oakland City Journal, 1907.

Dillon, John B. *A History of Indiana.* Indianapolis: Bingham and Doughty, 1859.

Dunn, Jacob P. Jr. *Indiana: A Redemption from Slavery*. New and enlarged edition. Boston: Houghton Mifflin, 1905.

———. *Indiana and Indianans: A History of Aboriginal and Territorial Indiana and the Century of Statehood*. 5 vols. Chicago: American Historical Society, 1919.

Esarey, Logan, ed., *Messages and Letters of William Henry Harrison*. 2 vols. Indianapolis: Indiana Historical Commission, 1922.

———. *Messages and Papers of Jonathan Jennings, Ratliff Boon, William Hendricks, 1816–1825*. Indianapolis: Indiana Historical Commission, 1924.

Etcheson, Nicole. *The Emerging Midwest: Upland Southerners and the Political Culture of the Old Northwest, 1787–1861*. Bloomington, IN: Indiana University Press, 1996.

Goebel, Dorothy. *William Henry Harrison: A Political Biography*. Indianapolis: Historical Bureau of the Indiana Library and Historical Department, 1926.

Goodman, Paul, ed. *The Federalists vs. the Jeffersonian Republicans*. New York: Holt and Winston, 1967.

Govorchin, Gerald. "The Political Life of Jonathan Jennings, First Governor of Indiana." Master's thesis, University of Chicago, 1942.

Hall, James. *Letters from the West: Containing Sketches of Scenery, Manner, and Customs, and Anecdotes Connected with the First Settlements of the Western Sections of the United States*. 1828. Reprint, Gainesville, FL: Scholars' Facsimiles and Reprints, 1967.

History of Gibson County Indiana, with Illustrations Descriptive of Its Scenery, and Biographical Sketches of Some of Its Prominent Men and Pioneers. Edwardsville, IL: Jas. T. Tartt and Company, 1884.

Hopkins, James, and Mary W. M. Hargreaves, eds. *The Papers of Henry Clay*. 10 vols. Lexington, KY: University of Kentucky Press, 1959–92.

Jakle, John A. *Images of the Ohio Valley: A Historical Geography of Travel, 1740 to 1860*. New York: Oxford University Press, 1977.

Jennings, Eileen Stockman. *The Jennings Family: Descendants of David Jennings*. Marceline, MO: Walsworth Publishing Co., 1976.

Lewis, Peirce. "American Roots in Pennsylvania Soil." In E. Willard Miller, ed., *A Geography of Pennsylvania*. University Park, PA: Pennsylvania State University Press, 1995.

Lindley, Harlow, ed. *Indiana as Seen by Early Travelers: A Collection of Reprints from Books of Travel, Letters, and Diaries Prior to 1830*. Indianapolis: Indiana Historical Bureau, 1916.

Madison, James. *The Indiana Way: A State History*. Bloomington: Indiana University Press; Indianapolis: Indiana Historical Society, 1986.

Marryat, Frederick. *A Diary in America, with Remarks on Its Institutions*. New York: Knopf, 1962.

McCord, Shirley S., ed. *Travel Accounts of Indiana, 1679–1961: A Collection of Observations by Wayfaring Foreigners, Itinerants, and Peripatetic Hoosiers*. Indianapolis: Indiana Historical Bureau, 1970.

Morrison, Mabel C. *Ann Gilmore Hay: Wife of Jonathan Jennings, from 1811–1826*. Indianapolis: John E. Hampton, 1925.

Nowland, John H. B. *Sketches of Prominent Citizens of 1876: With a Few of the Pioneers of the City and County Who Have Passed Away*. Indianapolis: Tilford and Carlon, 1877.

Power, Richard Lyle. *Planting Corn Belt Culture: The Impress of the Upland Southerner and Yankee in the Old Northwest*. Indianapolis: Indiana Historical Society, 1953.

Ralston, Samuel. "Jonathan Jennings, First Governor of Indiana." In *Proceedings of the Third Annual Conference on Indiana History*. Bulletin No. 15 (February 1922).

Riker, Dorothy L., comp. *Unedited Letters of Jonathan Jennings*. Indianapolis: Indiana Historical Society, 1932.

Riker, Dorothy L., and Gayle Thornbrough, comps. *Indiana Election Returns, 1816–1851*. Indianapolis: Indiana Historical Bureau, 1960.

Robertson, Nellie Armstrong, and Dorothy L. Riker, eds. *The John Tipton Papers*. 3 vols. Indianapolis: Indiana Historical Bureau, 1942.

Rorabaugh, W. J. *The Alcoholic Republic: An American Tradition.* New York: Oxford University Press, 1979.

Smith, Brent. "The Biography of Jonathan Jennings: Indiana's First Governor." Ph.D. diss., Ball State University, 1987.

Smith, Oliver H. *Early Indiana Trials and Sketches: Reminiscences.* Cincinnati: Moore, Wilstach, Keys and Company, 1858.

Sweet, William Warren. *Revivalism in America: Its Origin, Growth, and Decline.* Gloucester, MA: Peter Smith, 1965.

Thomson, Gladys Scott. *A Pioneer Family: The Birkbecks in Illinois, 1818–1827.* London: Jonathan Cape, 1953.

Thornbrough, Gayle, ed. *The Correspondence of John Badollet and Albert Gallatin, 1804–1836.* Indianapolis: Indiana Historical Society, 1963.

———. *The Diary of Calvin Fletcher.* 9 vols. Indianapolis: Indiana Historical Society, 1972–83.

Thornbrough, Gayle, and Dorothy L. Riker, eds. *Journals of the General Assembly of Indiana Territory, 1805–1815.* Indianapolis: Indiana Historical Bureau, 1950.

Thornbrough, Mary Lou. *The Negro in Indiana: A Study of a Minority.* Indianapolis: Indiana Historical Bureau, 1957.

Tocqueville, Alexis de. *Democracy in America.* 2 vols. New York: Alfred A. Knopf, 1963.

Trollope, Frances. *Domestic Manners of the Americans.* Ed. David Smalley. New York: Alfred A. Knopf, 1949.

Thwaites, Ruben Gold, ed. *Early Western Travels.* Cleveland, OH: Arthur H. Clark Company, 1905.

Twining, Thomas. *Travels in America 100 Years Ago.* New York: Harper and Brothers, 1894.

Walsh, Justin E. *The Centennial History of the Indiana General Assembly, 1816–1978.* Indianapolis: The Select Committee on the Centennial History of the Indiana General Assembly, 1987.

Wheeler, Adade Mitchell, and Marlene Stein Wortman. *The Roads They Made: Women in Illinois History.* Chicago: Charles H. Keen Publishing Co., 1977.

Woollen, William. *Biographical and Historical Sketches of Early Indiana.* Indianapolis: Hammond and Company, 1883.

Wright, John Stillman. *Letters from the West, or, a Caution to Emigrants: Being Facts and Observations Respecting the States of Ohio, Indiana, Illinois, and Some Parts of New York, Pennsylvania, and Kentucky*. Salem, NY: Dodd and Stevenson, 1819.